Chew Magna
May 2015.

FROM SOMERSET TO THE PYRENEES

IN THE STEPS OF

THE REVEREND WILLIAM ARTHUR JONES

GEOLOGIST AND ANTIQUARY

Somerset Archaeological
& Natural History Society

The Reverend William Arthur Jones c.1860
(Somerset Archaeological and Natural History Society)

From Somerset to the Pyrenees
in the Steps of
The Reverend William Arthur Jones
Geologist and Antiquary

David Rabson

with many thanks for your help and encouragement

David Rabson

18 June 2015 *

Après l'étude de Dieu et du coeur humain, la contemplation de la nature dans ses magnifiques aspects peut être considérée comme l'une de nos plus douces jouissances, et l'un de nos devoirs les plus saints.

Émilien Frossard (1802-1881)
Pasteur et Pyrénéiste

* 200th anniversary of the Battle of Waterloo

Somerset Archaeological and
Natural History Society

The quotation on the title page can be translated as:

'After the study of God and of the human heart the contemplation of nature in its magnificent aspects can be considered one of our sweetest pleasures and one of our most holy duties.'[1]

Cover illustrations:

Front: Le Cirque de Gavarnie, Hautes-Pyrénées (from an old postcard)
Back: Taunton Castle in 1839 (SANHS)

The Somerset Archaeological and Natural History Society (SANHS) was founded in 1849 and purchased Taunton Castle in 1874 which has been the home of the Society ever since. The Society is a registered charity who have been publishing and preserving Somerset's heritage since 1849

The views expressed in this volume are those of the author and not those of the Somerset Archaeological and Natural History Society

Typeset in Garamond
Typeset and designed by David Worthy and Adrian Webb
Printed by Short Run Press, Exeter

ISBN 978 0 902152 28 1

CONTENTS

Foreword vi

Introduction and Acknowledgements vii

Chapter 1 – Growing up in Carmarthen 1

Chapter 2 – Bridgend 9

Chapter 3 – University days in Glasgow 14

Chapter 4 – First contacts with Somerset 20

Chapter 5 – Northampton 23

Chapter 6 – Somerset 34

Chapter 7 – The Somerset Archaeological and Natural History Society 40

Chapter 8 – Two years in the Pyrenees 50

Chapter 9 – The return to Taunton 77

Chapter 10 – Civic activities 80

Chapter 11 – Arthur Jones's religious views 84

Chapter 12 – Last days 86

Chapter 13 – Postscript 91

Bibliography 93

Appendices 95

References 105

Subscribers 109

Foreword

A GREAT FLOWERING OF INTEREST in archaeology, local history, and the natural environment took place in early Victorian England. One of its most enduring legacies was the foundation of county societies devoted to furthering such interests. The Somerset Archaeological and Natural History Society was typical of the movement. Founded in 1849 after discussions among 'several gentlemen of Taunton and its neighbourhood', it attracted keen interest from large numbers of Somerset gentry and clergy. After two years it had over four hundred members and published the first volume of its annual Proceedings. A start had also been made in collecting items for a museum and books for a small library. The Society we cherish today grew on these foundations.

It was a happy accident that in the same year that the SANHS was founded, a 31-year old Unitarian minister, the Revd William Arthur Jones, moved from Northampton to Somerset. After three years he made a crucial shift from Bridgwater's Dampiet Street to Taunton's Mary Street Unitarian Chapel. Given his antiquarian interests, he was soon drawn in to the local affairs of the new Society. He was to serve as its honorary secretary, and as a contributor to its research and its collections. Until his death in 1873 he was to be a major influence on shaping the Society. A monument to his memory stands in the grounds of Taunton Castle.

In this pioneering biography, David Rabson unravels the complex threads in Jones's life. He traces how the son of a Carmarthen tradesman went on to study in Wales and Scotland before taking up the Unitarian ministry in the Midlands. He shows how Jones became a central figure in Somerset mid-Victorian life, steering the Society, founding a school of science and art in Taunton, chairing the Taunton and Somerset Hospital committee, and backing liberal causes throughout the locality. Generous to public causes with his energy and time, he was recalled as a man with "a kindness of heart and amenity of manner which endeared him to all who had the pleasure of knowing him".

Jones is blessed to have as his biographer David Rabson. David studied in Cambridge under the formidable Somerset-born geographer Professor Richard Chorley and went on to qualify as a professional planner, coming to Somerset in 1978 to work for the Exmoor National Park Authority. As with Jones the county worked its spell on him and he became deeply immersed in Somerset through his work on Exmoor, his study of the Sanford family and of his home parish of Nynehead, and in the work of SANHS. Here he has pieced together from many disparate archival sources the life of one of the Society's early statesman.

As a son of the parsonage, the author empathizes with Jones's religious as well as his scientific views and presents a rounded picture of a complex and sometimes contradictory character. His skill in handling the French archives also allows him to throw new light on Jones' two years in France. In all his research, David has been greatly aided by the support of his wife Sheila and by the encouragement of friends within the Society. We all sit on the shoulders of those who worked so hard to shape what we too often take for granted. Here at last is a fine memorial to one of Somerset's founding intellectual fathers: William Arthur Jones deserves nothing less.

Peter Haggett
Emeritus Professor of Geography, University of Bristol

Introduction

O N 9 JULY 1838 the 20 year old William Arthur Jones bade farewell to his family and friends in his home town of Carmarthen in south west Wales and set off on the 45 mile walk to his brother John's home in Bridgend in Glamorganshire. Thirty five years later his funeral in the Somerset town of Taunton was a major event: crowds lined the streets and the town's two MPs came down from London for the occasion. Local papers ran long complimentary obituaries. When reporting, in the autumn of 1873, a proposal to establish a memorial to him the *Taunton Courier* commented that 'No man in this place, probably, during the last twenty years, has contributed more efficiently to those local institutions which mark the higher civilisation of a town'.[2] A memorial was erected at Taunton Castle to mark his contribution to the work of the Somerset Archaeological and Natural History Society and by the end of the century he had been given an entry in the *Dictionary of National Biography*.[3]

My interest in Arthur Jones was started by a chance find that I made in the papers of the Sanford family of Nynehead Court in Somerset, held in the Somerset Heritage Centre in Taunton. In 1867 Jones wrote three letters to William Ayshford Sanford. What made the letters stand out was firstly where they were written - the towns of Pau and Argelès-de-Bigorre in the French Pyrenees – and, secondly, their content. As well as describing his family's life during their two-year stay in the Pyrenees in 1866-1868, Jones talks about his scientific activities and his contacts with members of the Société Ramond, a Pyrenean counterpart of the Somerset Archaeological and Natural History Society.[4] The letters are of particular interest to me because of my contacts with the Pyrenees. These began in 1993 when staff from the Parc National des Pyrénées visited Exmoor, where I was working for the National Park Authority.

Although the two years that Jones spent in the south of France were the starting point for my research it soon expanded to cover all of his 55 years. While I have concentrated on his antiquarian and natural history interests the book also covers, although more briefly, his contribution to the communities in which he lived, including his work as a Unitarian minister. Jones lived through a time of great social, economic and scientific change which included the coming of the railways and the publication of Charles Darwin's *On the Origin of Species*. It is clear also that he was a great lover of the outdoors and travel and his papers are full of descriptions of journeys he made, both for leisure and of necessity. Much more could be written therefore about his civic and religious activities and I hope that my account encourages further exploration of these aspects of his life.

Because there is no single comprehensive set of Jones papers my research has drawn on a wide range of sources. The most fruitful sources of information are in the Somerset Heritage Centre (particularly the Farewell Jones papers, the archives of the Sanford family of Nynehead Court in Somerset, the papers of the Somerset Archaeological and Natural History Society and the Society's *Proceedings*), and the privately-owned Blake archives. As will be seen some of the most detailed information comes from two diaries kept by the young Arthur Jones for part of his time at the Carmarthen College and at Glasgow University.[5] It would be surprising if these were the only diaries that he wrote – perhaps the missing ones are out there somewhere! Where possible I have allowed Jones's own words, and those of his family and friends, to tell his story but in his diaries and his letters the handwriting is not always clear. From time to time therefore I have had recourse to interpolations [. . .] to make sense of what he wrote or to explain particular words. I have referred to Jones as 'Arthur' as he usually signed letters as 'W. Arthur Jones' and I believe the use of the second Christian name was the Welsh custom.

Acknowledgements

THE RESEARCH FOR THIS BOOK has taken me in person to places as varied as West Wales, Northampton, London and the Pyrenees, and (electronically) to Canada, Scotland and Massachusetts, and would not have been possible without the help of many people, in particular the late W. Seymour Blake of South Petherton (great-grandson of Arthur Jones), who kindly allowed me free use of the Blake family archives; the staff of the Somerset Heritage Centre and the Museum of Somerset in Taunton and of the public archives in Carmarthen, Bridgend, Northampton, Bagnères-de-Bigorre and Pau, and of the Glasgow University Archives; François and Marie-Paule Mengelle of the Société d'Etudes des Sept Vallées Lavedan, Argelès-Gazost; and Agnès Mengelle, Curator of the Musée Pyrénéen, Lourdes.

I am particularly grateful for the encouragement I have received from Tom Mayberry; from Dr Adrian Webb of the SANHS Publications Committee, who read an early draft, provided one of the maps, drew the Arthur Jones family tree, helped design this book and guided me through the publication process; Professor Peter Haggett, who also read an early draft and kindly agreed to provide the Foreword; Mary Siraut and David Bromwich who read a final version of the text and helped with the illustrations; David Worthy for helping to design the book and for his guidance with the illustrations; my friend Chantal Verdier of the Parc National des Pyrénées, who introduced me to this amazing area; and, not least, from my wife Sheila for her help and forbearance and in particular for checking the final version of the text.

My thanks are also due to the Maltwood Fund for a grant towards the cost of the research. Summerfield Developments contribution to the publication costs is also gratefully acknowledged. The company's headquarters are at Tauntfield, South Road, Taunton, the house where the Revd W.A. Jones spent his last years.

THE FAMILY TREE OF WILLIAM ARTHUR JONES

SHOWING THE CONNECTIONS BY MARRIAGE BETWEEN THE JONES AND BLAKE FAMILIES

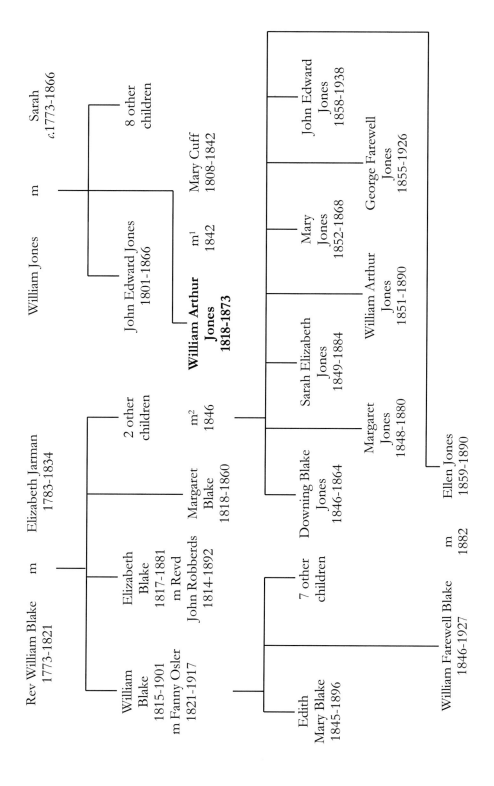

1.1: Arthur Jones's home town of Carmarthen in 1834. The Heol Awst chapel (1) lies on the south side of Lammas Street, the broad thoroughfare west of the town centre. The Jones family lived on Lammas Street. Behind the chapel lies its 'burying ground', which backs onto Friars Park, the site of Civil War earthworks. The historic core of the town, around the castle, overlooks the River Tywi in the south east corner of the map. (Extract from a map held by the Carmarthenshire Archive Service)

Chapter One
Growing up in Carmarthen

W ILLIAM ARTHUR JONES was born on 1 May 1818 in the market town of Carmarthen in the south west of Wales. The town is at the centre of a rich agricultural area comprising hills to the north, the wide valley of the River Tywi and lowlands stretching south to the coast. The historic core of the town is perched on a bluff on the north bank of the river, which rises in central Wales and flows into the Bristol Channel 12 miles to the south west. Historically Carmarthen had always been an important centre. In Roman times it was the town of Moridunum. In the Middle Ages it was the site of the largest Franciscan friary in Wales, dating from the thirteenth century, while just outside the town, at Abergwili, was the bishop's palace, now the County Museum. By the end of the fifteenth century Carmarthen had become the largest town in Wales and the centre of the King's administration. The English Civil War also left its mark in the form of earthworks in Friars Park to the south west of the town centre.

By 1800 the town's role had diminished but it remained the county town of Carmarthenshire, with a population of 9,995 in 1831. A 'Plan of Carmarthen' in 1834, held in the Carmarthen Record Office, shows that at its heart were the remains of the mediaeval castle housing the county gaol. The castle was one of many in the area including Dynevor and Dryslwyn, both looking over the Vale of Tywi upstream from the town.

The 1834 map also shows that the town's agricultural importance was reflected in its markets and 80 public houses, inns and hotels. As well as the parish church of St Peter and a site for a new Anglican church, there was a strong nonconformist tradition, with five chapels: the Independent Heol Awst in Lammas Street, with its own burial ground; Methodist (Upper Water); English Wesleyan (Chapel Place); Welsh Wesleyan (Cambrian Place) and the Tabernacle (Tabernacle Row). There were a Free Grammar School and separate National Schools for boys and girls. On the edge of the town were a 'gass' (*sic*)

works, an armoury and a brickworks, but as yet no railway: this did not reach the town until 1852 when the South Wales Railway was extended westwards from Swansea to Neyland, west of Carmarthen.

The Jones family (not surprisingly one of many of that name in the town, which could make life difficult for the researcher) were members of the Heol Awst chapel of which Arthur's father, William Jones senior, was a deacon.

1.2: Lammas Street, Carmarthen, looking west. The Heol Awst Chapel is on the left. (Author's Collection (AC))

The chapel is situated on the south side of Lammas Street, a broad thoroughfare to the west of the town centre; behind the chapel lies its burial ground. Established on the present site in about 1715, broadly in the Presbyterian tradition, the chapel building of 1726 had to be rebuilt in 1802 to serve a growing congregation. It was receiving a new lease of life under the renowned dissenting minister David Peter and was developing a Congregational

1.3: Heol Awst Chapel, Lammas Street. (AC)

and Trinitarian persuasion, which led to some Unitarians leaving. Despite this the congregation grew rapidly and by 1826 the chapel had to be rebuilt yet again to accommodate an even greater number of worshippers. A new schoolroom was added in the late nineteenth century between the chapel and the street.[6]

Arthur Jones was the youngest child of William and Sarah Jones. It is not known precisely when William senior was born and died but it is recorded that he died when Arthur was young, probably in the 1820s. There is conflicting evidence about his occupation. Arthur Jones's entry in the *Dictionary of National Biography* (originally written by George Farewell Jones, one of his sons) says William senior was a corn merchant, a statement repeated in 1901 in a list of Unitarian students at the Carmarthen College.[7] However, the Heol Awst baptism register lists ten children of a William Jones (cooper) and Sarah Jones, including a William Arthur, baptised on 10 May 1818.[8] Some of the other children's names agree with those mentioned in Arthur's diary. In addition William Jones (cooper) is one of the signatories on a deed of trust for land for the burial place for the chapel, dated 4 February 1813.[9] Pigot's Street Directory of 1822 also lists a William Jones, cooper, of Lammas Street but has no corn merchant of the same name. William is not in the 1830 edition of the same directory, all of which suggests that Arthur Jones' father was indeed a cooper although it is conceivable that he was also a corn merchant in a small way. Sarah Jones outlived her husband by many years, at first living in Lammas Street, being recorded in the 1851 Census of Population as 'head of household/annuitant'. She later moved to be with her son John in Bridgend where she died on 3 April 1863 at the age of 93.[10]

The Heol Awst baptism register records that William and Sarah's ten children started with James, born in 1797: by the time William Arthur was born in 1818, the youngest by seven years, the family consisted of five boys and four girls. Surprisingly there is little in Arthur Jones's diaries about his family apart from occasional references, his relationship with his brother John Edward, born in 1801, being the exception. Little else is known about Arthur Jones's early childhood. It is likely that he followed his brother John to the school set up by David Peter after which, in 1834, at the age of 16, he took a place at the Carmarthen Presbyterian College of which David Peter was the Principal. This had been set up in 1704 to train Presbyterian ministers but also accepted other Dissenting students

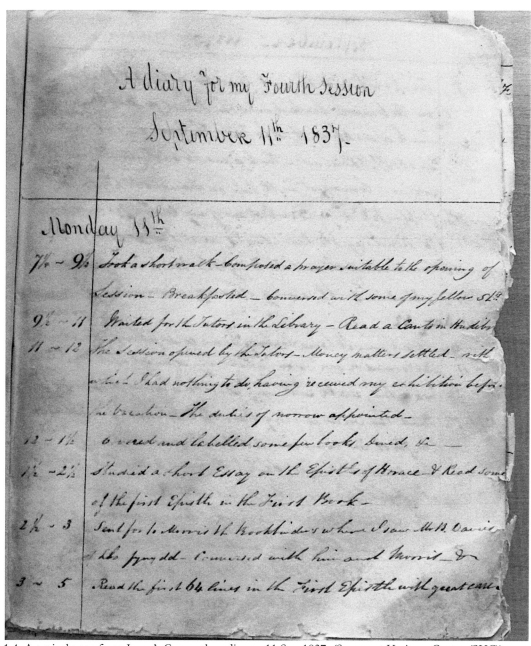

1.4: A typical page from Jones's Carmarthen diary – 11 Sep 1837. (Somerset Heritage Centre (SHC))

including those destined for the Unitarian ministry. Jones would have lived at home while at the college, as it occupied the lecture room and the library at the Heol Awst chapel before moving to another site in the town in 1835.[11]

The first detailed account of Arthur Jones's life comes in the diary he kept for his last year at the college, from September 1837 to July 1838. In this he describes both his academic work and his other activities. Although he spoke both English and Welsh it was written in English, suggesting that it was his first language. However, on many occasions he did use the local tongue, as on Sunday 19 September 1837 when, after breakfast, he walked six miles to 'Gelly' (probably Gellywen) to the north west of Carmarthen, where he preached in Welsh. On another occasion he records that he 'Read Lardner on the Two Epistles to the Thessalonians [*presumably in Greek*] . . . Read the first 3 chapters of the First Epistle, noting the translation very seldom and then only the Welsh one'. Ability to read and write in different languages was important for Jones. His studies for the ministry at the Carmarthen College and later at Glasgow University required him also to be conversant with Latin, Greek and Hebrew, an interest in languages which is reflected in work he did much later in Somerset.

While the diary concentrates on his life at the college, his interests in geology and natural history and his excursions, it does reveal other aspects of his life. In the late 1830s the temperance movement was just beginning in the Carmarthen area; Jones was not unaffected and indeed there was a moment when he was tempted to go down that route. On 7 February 1838 he attended an evening service at the Methodist Water Street Chapel where he heard 'the most eloquent discourse I ever heard on any subject, delivered . . . by Mr. Grubbs in favour of total abstinence. [I was] much affected by the discourse and would almost say with Felix 'Almost thou hast persuaded me to be a [teetotaller]'. However he did not succumb and he often describes taking wine, as on 21 March when he called on Mr. Davies of Cwm near Carmarthen 'where I was obliged to take a glass of port and a biscuit'.

There are other insights into his character. He was a serious young man who was impatient with small talk. In recording a discussion with fellow students about England, the English, English manners and etiquette he comments that he had 'Spent the hour very <u>pleasantly</u> but <u>not</u> perhaps <u>profitably</u>. During this time I might almost have got my Hebrew lecture ready'. He was very methodical with a great attention to detail. In his diary he describes his activities not only by the date but also by the time of day, as in the very first entry, for Monday 11 September 1837:

7¼ - 9½	Took a short walk. Composed a prayer suitable to the opening of session
	Breakfasted. Conversed with some of my fellow students.
11-12	Meeting with tutors – not involved in discussion about money having received my exhibition before the vacation.
5-7	Studied first 4 chapters of the 22 Psalm in Hebrew.
9¼ -10¼	Transcribed one of my Welsh sermons.

The exhibition was a grant that Jones received from the Trust in London that had been set up in 1711 under the will of an earlier Welsh dissenter, Dr Daniel Williams. One of its main aims was to support the education of ministers in 'the Three Denominations' of Presbyterian, Congregational and Unitarian.[12]

Jones studied the full range of subjects then needed for the ministry but he also had many extra-curricular activities. With its fine countryside and many historic monuments the Carmarthen area was full of interest and it is clear that from this early stage of his life he was fascinated by local buildings, wildlife and landscape. He took an almost daily 'constitutional' in the town but often ventured further afield. Of necessity walking was a major part of his life, although he occasionally borrowed a pony. In future years he was able to travel by train and canal but his pleasure in walking stayed with him throughout his life. His youngest son John remembered at the end of the century that 'Father held that a person should be able to walk a mile for each year of age'.[13] His diary records several long excursions. On 9 June 1838 he set off on a three-day walk of about 40 miles eastwards up the valley of the River Tywi:

> 9/6 Walked to Llandilo by 6½. Called at Mr. J. Charles. Afterwards walked to Plas Bach, 3 miles distant. Found the Edwardses all well.
>
> 10/6 Preached at Llandyfaen in the morning. Attendance thin in consequence of the weather. Felt quite exhausted after the service from exertion in preaching and leading the singing. The old minister Mr. Griffiths present. Returned to Plas Bach. Raining all day. Kept within doors. In the evening took a walk over the farm.
>
> 11/6 Returned home through Golden Grove Park. Walked around the Mansion. Enjoyed the most splendid view from the top of the hill above the Mansion, commanding the Vale of Towy up to Llandovery and down to Carmarthen, just above the noble grounds of Dynevawr Park. The characteristic of the scene was softness. Well wooded and beautifully ornamented by the graceful windings of the Towy. Went to Llanfyhangel churchyard. Found all the people in the neighbourhood enjoying this day on which Lord Emlyn, the heir of G. Grove, comes of age. Walked to Llanarthey. Here I took some bread and cheese and read 3 of the Eps of Horace Book I. From thence to Carmarthen where I arrived about 3.

The mansion at Golden Grove (now known as Gelli Aur and surrounded by a country park) is a somewhat sombre grey building, with splendid views northwards across the Tywi valley. At the time of Jones's visit it was a relatively new feature in the landscape, having been built between 1827 and 1830 to replace a sixteenth century mansion for the Cawdor family. The architect was Jeffrey Wyattville, who had worked on many commissions throughout the country including work at Windsor Castle and the 'makeover', in modern parlance, of Sidney Sussex College in Cambridge (where the author spent three mostly enjoyable years in the 1960s). The design for the tower at Golden Grove is remarkably similar to that of the gatehouse at the college.

Many of Jones's diary entries reveal an appreciation of landscape, as in this record of

1.5: The Tywi valley looking west from Dryslwyn Castle. (AC)

a visit to the country to the north west of Carmarthen. On Saturday 14 October he walked to 'Pantrafle' (possibly present day Blaentrafle) 15 miles north of the town, retiring to bed after supper by 9.30 p.m.. The following morning he rose early and was out and about before breakfast:

> ¼ 7 – 8   Took a long walk in the neighbouring dell which was highly romantic, one side thickly wooded with fir, the other barren except here and there a plot of furze. The bottom of the valley was traversed by a noisy brooklet which now beat furiously against its rocky structures then glided gently and without a dimple on its face but that was for a short time for it shortly rushed into the underwood and wound its way unseen yet not unheard. Had a good appetite for breakfast when I returned. Preached in the morning to a very numerous congregation at Rhydy Park. Returned to dinner with J. Philips Esq. at Pantrafle.
>
> 2 ¼ - 7   Rode for about 5 miles on Mr. Philips' little pony. Walked the remaining 10 miles to Carmarthen.

Other walks had more specific objectives. On one occasion, after attending a singing session at the chapel, he went out of the town to listen to a nightingale which was said to be there. Nothing was heard! On another he went into the country with Mr F.M. Davies to try out the accuracy of the latter's 'theodolet'. He attended a lecture at the town hall on astronomy and saw several objects magnified by the 'Oxy-Hydrogen microscope' such as a drop of water, the leg of a bee and a dragonfly's wing. Twenty years later he was to give his own talks on the application of the microscope to the investigation of natural history and archaeology.[15]

However, his greatest interest seemed to be in geology and it was important to him that he could see features on the ground, to collect fossils and to explain them to others. So, on 15 September he walked a short distance to the south west of the town:

> With cl. fell. took a walk to a quarry on Penallty Knap. Found no organic remains. Observed that the strata were almost perpendicular, and in one place contorted as if by a great convulsion. The science of geology formed the subject of our conversation on our return. None of my cl. fell. had studied this science at all.[16]

Penallty Knapp, now known as Ystrad Wood, is the wooded end of a low ridge about a mile west of the town centre, rising to about 300 feet above sea level. Today, having entered the woodland at its northern end, one follows a narrow path through the wood eventually arriving in an overgrown quarry where near-vertical Ordovician strata up to

30 feet in height can be seen. There is evidence that stone has been quarried here since Roman times.

The 1830s were an exciting time for a 19 year-old with a serious interest in geology. The Bible–based accounts of the history of the earth were being challenged increasingly successfully and it was being accepted that the planet had not been created on 23 October 4004 BC, as calculated in 1650 by Bishop James Ussher. The Earth was being subjected to description and classification as never before, with particular interest being

1.7: Ordovician strata at Penallty Knapp (Ystrad Wood), Carmarthen. (AC)

taken in fossils. In 1815, a few years before Jones was born, William Smith had published his geological map of England and Wales. Charles Lyell's three volume *Principles of Geology* was published between 1831 and 1833, and on the Dorset coast Mary Anning was finding and selling ichthyosaur fossils.

In Wales Roderick Impey Murchison was working on his Silurian study, which included the geology of Carmarthenshire. He made several visits to the area in the early 1830s, obtaining information from landowners and professional men such as Lord Dynevor and John Bowen MD. It is quite possible that Jones came to hear of this during his many walks around the area. In addition, one of the subscribers to Murchison's book was Dr James Yates F.G.S. (1789-1871) who had studied at Glasgow University. He was a Fellow of the Geological Society, the Linnean Society and the Royal Society, and was appointed secretary to the Council of the British Association for the Advancement of Science in 1831. He was also a Trustee of the Dr Williams Foundation and was very much Jones's mentor, so it is likely that some of his interests had influenced the young Arthur.[17]

Jones benefited greatly from the Carmarthen College library, which held many books dating back to the beginning of the eighteenth century, including such works as Whiston's *Theory of the Earth* (1708), Woodward's *Earth and Minerals* (1702) and Burnett's *Theory of the Earth* (1722).[18] He also made great use of the *Penny Cylopedia* and *Penny Magazine*, published by the wonderfully named Society for the Diffusion of Useful Knowledge. The *Cyclopedia* was a multi-volume encyclopedia issued between 1833 and 1843 while the *Magazine* appeared every Saturday from March 1832 to October 1845. They were designed to bring developments in science and related matters to the working classes in an inexpensive form. Jones also had a few geological books of his own, including William Buckland's *Bridgewater Treatises*.

The entries in his diary show how Jones was quite happy to accept the new thinking and how much time he devoted to books on scientific matters. His critical approach to what he was reading must have been a reflection of his independent religious up-bringing in which freethinking was encouraged: it is noteworthy that scientists with a Unitarian background included Joseph Priestley and Charles Darwin.

On 27 September he 'Read scraps on geology in the *Penny Magazine*' and 'Explained to (the Davies?) the fossil specimens of the ammonites and *nautili* which I presented to them, and gave them an outline of geology'. On the following day he 'read some pieces in the library' and 'pored over a great many of the old books'. He was 'amused by the curious explanations given of fossil skeletons in an old Natural History'. 29 September saw him reading different articles in the *Penny Cyclopedia* and studying the articles on geology 'very carefully' while a day later he tackled 'Ray's proof of the Deluge'.[19]

> A curious old work. What confused and obscure notions they had of the formation of the crust of the Earth. What appears difficult to Ray, is now quite clear from the modern science of geology.

Jones's interests were not confined to geology. At various times he records that he had *inter alia* explained the nature of quadratics to a fellow student; practised some old psalm tunes; studied Voltaire and Locke on Toleration and collected caddis fly larvae in a local river.

He took his last exams at the College at the beginning of July 1838, and on 5 July had supper with fellow students which he chaired as being first in the class. It was not an event entirely of post-examination merriment. The party was joined by the Revd Davison and a Mr Lloyd from London, and an intense discussion ensued on such matters as the relative merits of monarchical and republican government, in the course of which the direction of Jones's political inclinations became clear. He commented in his diary: 'the latter of which [*i.e. republicanism*] I supported in opposition to the objections brought on by Mr Davison'; it might be that Jones was taking this line for the sake of argument, but in the light of his later political views this is unlikely. On the following day he received the half-yearly exhibition of £10 and a present of £4 15s from the Tutor. After chapel on the Sunday he called on Dr Jenkins, with whom he sat down for some time, and took wine with Mr Lloyd. Two days later he left the College and Carmarthen, to return only occasionally, although for a time he kept in contact with the College, in June 1844 assisting in the examination of the students.[20]

1.8: Trilobite collected by Jones at Llandeilo. (Carmarthenshire Museum on loan from the Museum of Somerset)

Chapter Two
Bridgend

AFTER FAREWELLS TO FAMILY AND FRIENDS, Arthur Jones left Carmarthen on 9 July 1838 for Bridgend in the Vale of Glamorgan to stay with his brother, the Revd John Jones. John was almost 17 years older than Arthur. He had also studied at the college in Camarthen but on leaving in 1821 had gone directly into the Unitarian ministry rather than to university, taking charge of both the English-speaking congregation at Bridgend (actually at Newcastle on the west side of the river) and the Welsh-speaking chapel at Bettws, a few miles to the north. Bridgend played an important role in Arthur's life at this time. He stayed with his brother during university vacations, and from this temporary home explored the wealth of historical and natural interest provided by the town and the surrounding area

In the 1830s Bridgend (in Welsh 'Pen-y-bont ar Ogwr') was a small market town on the River Ogmore in the parish of Coity, about 5 miles from the Bristol Channel. It was similar to Carmarthen in several respects: a twelfth century castle (Newcastle) was situated on the west side of the River; Ewenny priory, a Benedictine foundation dating from 1141, lay 1½ miles to the south; nearby to the east were the ruins of Coity Castle, a mediaeval fortress that had been abandoned in the sixteenth century. In 1838 the area had not yet received the full force of the industrial revolution and the rise of coal mining and steel making which became so important to the South Wales economy. Coal had been mined in Glamorgan in the thirteenth century but on a small scale, and by the 16th and 17th centuries the Neath area, a few miles to the northwest, was the focus of mining in this part of South Wales. However, mining in the valleys to the northeast, including the Rhondda, Merthyr and Aberdare, did not get going in a serious way until the 1840s although the iron and steel industry had been developing there since the eighteenth century and the population was growing rapidly. Communications in south Wales were generally were difficult. The railway did not reach the area until the 1840s and, apart from the main routes through the Vale of Glamorgan, roads were poor if not absent; Bridgend was not on a main road until 1832.

2.1: The Revd John Jones's chapel at Newcastle, Bridgend. (AC)

Arthur Jones walked the 45 miles from Carmarthen to Bridgend via Swansea, where he stayed two nights at the Golden Lion. He was accompanied by a friend, Mr D. Evans, and a pony belonging to a Mr Brocke, which made the journey easier; he does not say whether the pony carried one of them or just their luggage. On 10 July it was raining heavily and they were pressed to stay to visit the Swansea museum. This journey would have been familiar to Jones. He had already visited his brother that April when he had walked over to Bridgend from Carmarthen, staying one night at Cwm Mawr and one in Swansea. On that visit he took another of his long walks. On 15 April 1838, three days after arriving at Bridgend, he preached in English at the Newcastle chapel, then walked via Bettws up into the hills – 'through the most dramatic part of Glamorgan' - to 'Danyfel' (possibly Pen-y-foel). The next day he walked over the 1300 feet high Cefngwyngl to Aberdare, 16 miles to the north east of Bridgend as the crow flies. On the way he 'suffered from a very heavy snowstorm on the bleakest part of the mountain' and reached Aberdare at about 3 p.m. The following four days saw him walking a further four miles to Merthyr, then back into the Vale to Neath, arriving there on 20 April.

Jones spent July and August 1838 at Bridgend pursuing his studies and 'as an amusement' studying geology and collecting fossils. He also spent time with friends, visited the seaside and assisted at the school in Bridgend run by his brother. The contribution that John and Arthur had made to the local community was recognised in a memoir published in the *Bridgend and Neath Chronicle* in 1890:

> The Rev. John Jones, Unitarian minister, kept the best school in town and undoubtedly he and his brother, Mr William Jones, (who went on to Edinburgh [*actually Glasgow*] and afterwards became a very popular Unitarian minister) were as good scholars as any in Wales at that time. [21]

A 'Descriptive Essay' that Jones wrote in April 1839 at university shows one way in which he spent his leisure time.[22] It gives an account of a walk that he took, probably in the previous summer, in the hills to the east and north of the town, visiting among other places Coity Castle. The essay might of course have been a product of his imagination rather than the description of a walk actually made, but nevertheless he did know the area well. On the walk he was accompanied by an unnamed English friend.[23]

A Walk near Bridgend

From Llangreilo (Cowchurch in English) Jones and his companion walked up 'a most natural glen' enclosed on both sides by 'gently rising hillocks whose tops were crowned with the green foliage of a wood blooming in all the luxuriant loveliness of summer'. As already noted Jones's language often tends to be somewhat flowery, perhaps inspired by the Welsh bards, but here it clearly reveals his love of being out in the Welsh countryside:

> Oft when the summer sun set in its glory, casting a farewell glance on the fleecy clouds which seemed to mourn his departure, have we wandered through these fields and lived in realms which in our minds eye lay in the long fantastic range of clouds thickening in the West. And when our young heart was ready to burst with the little sorrows which we ourselves had caused, how often have we been soothed by the solitude of this calm retreat.

They soon reached the majestic ruins of the sixteenth century Coity castle:

> Hard by, stood the grey spire of the parish church rearing as it were the standard of peace over the fallen greatness of this once famous seat of War. A fair minute passed,

2.2: Coity Castle from an engraving by S. and N. Buck, 1740 (SANHS)

and we were beneath its walls. The moat was there, but it is now dry. The noble entrance which had once been defended by the strong portcullis, was now but a mockery of its former strength. The ruthless hand of Time had been aided in the work of destruction by the cupidity of some soulless neighbour; who, to save himself the trouble of quarrying, had used the beautifully chiseled stones to repair his stable! A watch-tower and many a high battlement still braved the storm and were oft the scene of daring enterprize to the village lads. To run along the upper wall -to stand on the dizzy height of yon tower - was the greatest glory to which the young Napoleons of the village ever aspired. This glory many a little urchin had acquired though on more occasions than one it was like to cost them their lives.

The ivy now creeps along the mouldering walls which once enclosed the spacious courtyard, in former days the scene of revelry and song or martial deeds of war. And even of late years the sound of music has not been unheard within these ruined walls, for upon festive days the happy youths of Coity have been known to dance on that greensward to violin and harp. There also many a feat of strength has been displayed by the village Hercules.

From Coity the walkers crossed a landscape where:

rich cornfields, highly cultivated meadows, fine fir groves and the river darkening and stealing away until the eye loses it in a forest (of) ancient oak, compose the fair picture of loveliness before our eyes. Immediately above this rose high and barren hills presenting one of those sudden transitions from the picturesque to the sublime in scenery not at all uncommon in Wales.

They dropped down into the valley of the River Ogmore which took them two miles upstream to Velin Ivan Dhû (Evan Dhû's Mill), 'a most romantic little spot'. The miller's house also served as the local inn where Jones and his companion, after spending some time looking round at the simple furniture, the books (including Bibles) and a map of the world, became more acquainted with the miller and his daughter:

Having finished our survey and done justice to the simple but substantial fare laid on the table, the landlord kindly consented to assist us in emptying the contents of a large measure of excellent cwrw (ale) which the pretty maid, miscalculating the bibulous capabilities of her strange guests, had laid before us.

After chatting for some time, partly in Welsh and partly in English, for my companion knew no Welsh, and the miller knew very little English, we took our leave of the host, not however without shaking his rosy cheeked daughter warmly by the hand and thanking her for her kind attention.

Surprisingly after such a repast the two companions were able to finish their walk with an hour's strenuous climb of the hill behind the inn from which magnificent views were obtained. The ridge, Mynydd Llangeinwyr, extends northwards between the Cwm Garw and Cwm Ogwr Fawr before culminating in the 1,864ft summit of Werfa on the county boundary, but Jones and his companion's climb ended at a lower summit, possibly Pen-y-Foel, 1,168ft in height, about 2½ miles to the north of the mill.

> We turned southward - the prospect was sublime. The whole expanse of the beautiful Vale of Glamorgan spread itself before us from Gwent to Neath.
>
> Dim in the far east rose the blue hills of Monmouth. Below them lay the town of Cardiff buried in surrounding wood – the Groves of Llandaff - the vast champaign reaching from Cardiff to Lantwit, once the famous seat of learning under the care of Iltudus, presented a fine sight.
>
> Far in the west on the other hand, was seen the beautiful Bay of Swansea, which is said to be the Bay of Naples in miniature. Between that and the mouth of the River Neath rose the bold hills of Briton Ferry, and towering above these the dim outline of the Black Mountains of Carmarthenshire and Brecon. From Aberavon eastward full thirteen miles lay the beautiful estate of Margam. Its fine forest, in which the ruins of the ancient abbey still stand, clothes the side of the hills at whose feet lies the finest corn country in Glamorgan.
>
> Immediately below us was the pretty little town of Bridgend with its picturesque and interesting scenery. The eye dwells with increased pleasure on the banks of the Ogmore which passes through the town, and loves to follow its devious windings until it empties itself into the Bristol Channel, which lay full before us, extending from the broadest part about Swansea to the mouth of the Avon which flows through Bristol. The Bristol steamers were plying on the sea in all directions. Here and there might be seen a small coasting skiff spreading all her canvas to the wind. We followed the tiny bark almost across until it was swallowed up in the haze which enveloped the shores of Somerset and Devon.

At the same time as helping his brother and exploring the Bridgend area, Jones was preparing to continue his education, now at Glasgow University, with the intention of entering the Unitarian ministry. The idea of going to Glasgow seems to have been suggested earlier in the year when his brother talked to him about his future. On 6 April 1838 he received a letter from his brother and Mr Thomas of Llandyssil which, as he 'pondered over the plans proposed by my brother' and 'read about Glasgow in the Penny Encyclopaedia', seems to have suggested a course of action.[24] The result was that in September he went up to London to stand an examination for one of Dr William's Glasgow Scholarships:

> I was one of six candidates for three scholarships, and so fortunate as to be placed first on the list of successful candidates, who were Mr. Jno Daniel Morell of Little Baddow in Essex, a nephew of Dr Morell and a student at Homerton of six years standing, and Mr. George Pridie from Halifax.

The Scholarships were provided by the Dr Williams Trust and had been established by James Yates in 1831 to provide financial support for men wishing to study for the Dissenting ministry at Glasgow University. There is no information on the content of the exams but it can be assumed that they included such subjects as Hebrew, Greek, Latin and biblical studies.

Jones's journey to London cannot have been straightforward, as there was not as yet a rail service from South Wales. By 1838 the Great Western line had reached Maidenhead from London and would take another three years to arrive at Bristol. The line between Swansea and Chepstow was not opened until 1850 and then to get to London one had to go via Gloucester. So how did Jones get to London? While the Kennet and Avon canal from Bristol to the Thames at Reading on a fly boat was possible it was a slow journey and did not serve as a long distance route. It would have been an unlikely choice.

Clues as to the routes customarily used are revealed in the diaries of the Revd Joseph Romilly who between 1827 and 1854 made several visits to Wales.[25] Coming from Cambridge via London in August of 1838 he made use of Brunel's Great Western Railway that had been opened to Maidenhead as recently as 4 June. This permitted the first part of the journey to Bristol to be done at a speed of 21 miles per hour rather than the 8 m.p.h. that a stagecoach could achieve. From the 1830s Bristol mail coaches went to Cardiff, Swansea and beyond via the difficult and potentially dangerous Old and New Passages across the Severn. The Old Passage crossed the estuary between Aust and Beachley while the New Passage followed roughly the line taken later by the Severn railway tunnel. The latter route was so difficult that from about 1830 the Old Passage was preferred. The engineer Thomas Telford commented in 1825 that the New Passage was

> one of the most forbidding places at which an important ferry crossing was ever established. It is, in truth, a succession of violent cataracts formed in a rocky channel, exposed to the rapid rush of a tide, which has scarcely an equal upon any other coast.[26]

One alternative was the boat service from Cardiff to Bristol that had been established in 1815, while some coach services avoided the Severn crossing entirely, taking the northerly route via Gloucester. From the 1840s such a service was available from Cardiff reaching London the same evening. Coach fares at that time were about 2p per mile although Jones did not have to worry about the cost as the London banker Mr Lloyd, who was associated with the Dr Williams Trust, had agreed to defray his expenses for the visit to London. Jones spent three weeks in the capital, 'very agreeably and profitably', staying with the Revd and Mrs Davison in Eaton Square. He visited his sister Anne, now living in Hatfield, before returning via the Dr Williams Trustees at their request. He found them 'very kind'. He also received from Mr Lloyd the 'handsome present' of £20 (the first instalment of his grant).

Chapter Three
University days in Glasgow

I N THE AUTUMN OF 1838 Arthur Jones left South Wales for Glasgow to take up
his place at the university. He was armed with a letter, dated 24 October, from Samuel
Cotton, secretary and solicitor to the Dr Williams Scholarship Trustees in London.[27] This
had originally been sent to Jones at Bridgend, with a note that it should reach him by 5
November, but was redirected to him at the home of the Revd George Harris, Unitarian
minister in Glasgow, arriving there on the morning of the 3 November. It gave detailed
and rigorous directions as to the course of study: 'You are required to enter as a Public
Student in the Logic or First Philosophy Class, and as such to wear the Gown, and to
obey the Laws of the University and follow the prescribed course'. The exhibition grant
of £30 per annum would be paid in two instalments but only if 'you discharge regularly
and diligently your duties as a Public Student, and you are not to absent yourself at any
time from the Lectures or Examinations, unless leave of absence be given you by the
Principal or by the Professors whom you attend'. The letter also makes it clear that the
aim of going to Glasgow was to carry out the studies needed to enter the Dissenting
ministry: not being a communicant member of the Church of England Jones could not
attend the ancient universities in England.

As we have seen Jones's main contact and mentor at the Dr Williams Foundation was
James Yates, who had been an un-ordained minister and had also studied at Glasgow
University. He kept in touch with Jones at Glasgow, giving him advice and, interestingly,
asking him to keep an eye on the welfare of fellow students. Jones attended the university
from 1838 to 1841, studying Ethics, Moral Philosophy, Classics, Hebrew, Elocution and
Mathematics, although according to university records the classes he attended were Logic
(1838-1839), Ethics (1839-1840) and Physics (1840-1841).

Jones's detailed diary for his time at Glasgow starts at the beginning of his second
year, in October 1839. It begins with a full description of his journey by sea from
Swansea. In 1840 there were only two railways in South Wales (the Swansea to
Oystermouth Railway and one from the valleys into Cardiff), neither of which was
connected to the then very sparse national network. Nor was there a railway from north
Lancashire to Glasgow: this was not started until 1845 in the railway mania of those years.
The favoured means for travel from South Wales to Scotland was therefore coastal packet.

At 5 a.m. on Wednesday 23 October Jones left Swansea on the *Mountaineer*, bound for
Liverpool. She was a 177 ton paddle steamer which also had two schooner-rigged masts.
She had been built by Patterson and Mercer of Bristol in 1835.[28] After a delay caused by
mechanical problems with the engine, which necessitated waiting in the Mumbles, the
ship eventually took shelter from a very heavy sea and a north east gale in St Bride's Bay.
Jones and other passengers took the opportunity to visit St David's, where 'we were all
highly delighted with the interiors of the Cathedral and the ruins of the Bishop's Palace'.
However, he was not impressed with the city of St David's itself which 'is now become
a mean dirty little village not worth visiting but for its antiquity'. He was not the only
person of this opinion. In August of the previous year the Revd Joseph Romilly had
visited the city and found it 'a collection of a few most miserable hovels'.[29]

The voyage took them across Cardigan Bay and round the Lleyn Peninsula and Anglesey, enabling Jones to reflect on the views of the Carnarvonshire mountains and on his emotional attachment to his native Wales.

> They certainly do present a most noble but I must confess a forbidding aspect. One's soul feels elevated, and swells with courageous pride, at the very thought that we are connected with them by birth. Nor is it a matter of surprise that those who lived amongst them should have so long and so successfully withstood the unwarrantable inroads of the haughty Romans in days of old, and of the Saxon invaders of more modern date.

The ship arrived at Liverpool in the middle of the night of Saturday 26 October when Jones seems to have been affected as much by the man-made as by the natural scene:

> . . . a thousand lamps sprang up in the distance standing like so many sentinels over the Metropolis of Commerce. As we drew nearer the grandeur of the scene was enhanced for the whole plain seemed studded with thousands of flaming stars which but for their regularity resembled those in the firmament of heaven.

In Liverpool he explored the city, including a visit to the Telegraph Office where he had 'the whole of the telegraph system explained', called on several acquaintances, went to a lecture at the Mechanics Institution and attended chapel twice on the Sunday; on the same journey a year later he attended a lecture on fossil remains given by 'Philips' (probably J.P. Phillips of the Ordnance Geological Survey). On the following morning he took the First Class train for Manchester on the railway which had been opened in September 1830. Here he visited and was impressed by the Museum of Natural History set up by the Manchester Natural History Society (founded in 1821) in Peter Street. Just as in Liverpool, he called on friends and attended chapel and a lecture, this time on geometry. He returned to Liverpool on the Tuesday morning, now travelling Second Class. His attention to detail and observation is shown by his diary entry, which notes that 'sometimes we travelled at the rate of two miles in 3 min. 55 secs': to measure the train's speed so accurately would have required both the use of a watch with a second hand and the presence of distance markers by the track. From Liverpool he took the

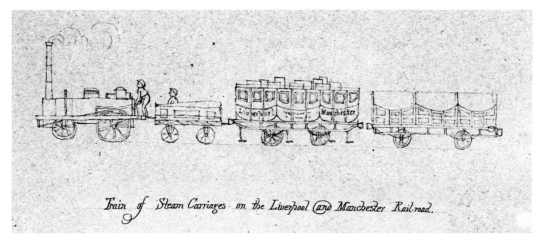

3.1: A train on the Liverpool to Manchester railway(sketch by Peter Orlando Hutchinson (1810-1897), antiquary, geologist and artist of Sidmouth, East Devon. (East Devon AONB/Devon Record Office)

3.2: Port Glasgow, 1830 from a sketch by Peter Orlando Hutchinson. (East Devon AONB/Devon Record Office)

Commodore Steam packet on an overnight voyage to Greenock, arriving at 10 a.m., from where 'at the expense of the Company we were carried up to Glasgow immediately in a smaller steamer'.

Where Arthur Jones lived during his first year in Glasgow is not known (perhaps at the home of the Unitarian minister the Revd Harris) but on arriving in October 1839 he took temporary lodgings in College Street. He spent Hallowe'en at Mr Harris's but a week later moved to Mrs Blair's at 283 High Street, also near the University. Here he pursued his academic studies, although not always with the application that was expected of him, as he revealed in a letter to his brother John the following January: 'I am rather concerned to find that my duties this session are much more severe than they were during the last. With all my exertions I find it impossible to do justice to all of the classes which I attend being by far the hardest working classes in College'.[30] The duties were indeed severe, if his diary record for Monday 18 November 1839 is typical, which reveals a timetable probably beyond the experience of most of today's students:

6 ½ -7 ½   Read the latter part of the 1 Ode in the iii of Horace and also a portion of the Second Epode.

7 ½ - 8 ½   Prof. Flemming commenced his lectures on sensation.

8 ½ - 9   Examined on Dactyllic Metres and finished Horace iii 1 Ode.

9 ½ - 10   Breakfasted. Looked over my mathematics.

10 – 11   Prof. Thomson established Art. 76 in his synopsis of Algebra.

11 – 12   Examination in Ethics.

12 – 1   Did some little business in town. Walked in College Green.

1 – 2   Prof. Ramsay continued his Prelectiones on Persius.

2 – 3 ½   Walked with Mr. Whitelegg. Read the papers & . . .

3 ½ - 4 ¼   Dined. Practised reading for the Elocution Class.

4 ½ - 8   Studied and transcribed my notes of the Prelectiones and also the observations made on Horace in the morning . . .

8 – 11   Studied Dr Thomson's Demonstration of Art. 75 &76 of his Synopsis. Transcribed my notes taken in the class room on the subject. The notes were full and copious.

11 – 12 ½   Studied the Choriambic Measures & read Horace for tomorrow.

Despite this heavy workload Jones was able to pursue his extra-curricular activities with enthusiasm. As at Carmarthen and Bridgend he took a great interest in the surrounding area and in particular its geology and history. He kept up his daily walks. He visited the Hunterian Museum, close to the university, taking in geological specimens from South Wales. From time to time he called on local ministers and preached for them. He also became politically active, joining the Liberal Association, becoming chairman of one of its committees and campaigning for the election of Sir John Herschel as Lord Rector.

He took the opportunity to see other parts of Scotland. On 26 December 1839 he left Port Dundas at Glasgow for Edinburgh, travelling overnight by a 'swift boat' on the Forth and Clyde Canal.[31] He arrived in the capital at 11 o'clock the following morning and spent his time exploring the city on foot and seeing the best known sights. He found the prospect from the South Bridge looking towards Prince's Street

> by far the most imposing I ever witnessed, especially at night. This was about 6 p.m. and the shop windows in Prince's Street were brilliantly lit up with gas and so stocked with goods of brightest hue as to resemble those gorgeous fairy palaces we read of in Eastern tales. And it appeared as though their foundations were in mid-air, hanging as it were over that deep and now dark hollow which lies between the South Bridge and the Mound.

He adds, somewhat prosaically: 'After tea went to the Theatre to see the Marriage of Figaro and the play of Guy Mannering'. On the following day he 'saw the whole of the Advocate's Library which is supposed to contain 170000 volumes, and is open to the public'. He was 'very much struck with a copy of the first printed bible, which was executed with wooden types in Germany' and by a 'still more curious and beautiful' manuscript bible in Latin, supposed to have belonged to King David I of Scotland.

In the spring of 1841 Jones explored the country around Glasgow and had crossed over eight counties. He had intended to visit the Isle of Arran, having learnt about its geology from John Pringle Nichol, Professor of Astronomy at the university, whom he

3.3: Edinburgh Castle from the Grass Market, October 1838 from a sketch by Peter Orlando Hutchinson. (East Devon AONB/Devon Record Office)

had met at the home of William Ramsay, the Professor of Humanity. Professor Nichol had conducted members of the British Association for the Advancement of Science over the island and Jones felt that he would be helpful in economising both time and labour on his visit. In his diary he makes two references to the Association, which held its annual meeting in Glasgow in September 1840. It is tempting to think that Jones attended the meeting but his diary for this month, if he made one, has not been found nor is there any reference to it in his letters.

There is no evidence that he did get to Arran and it seems unlikely, as on Wednesday 28 April he left Glasgow for a two day visit to explore the hills and lochs of the Trossachs, 20 miles to the north.[32] He travelled firstly by coach, crossing the remains of the Roman Antonine Wall just north of the city.[33] For the first few miles he saw nothing of interest but then the coach skirted the 'very rugged and uncouth form' of the Campsie Hills, and shortly after arrived at the village of Killearn, which provided a fine prospect of the lower part of Loch Lomond and its islands. At Balfron he left the coach and walked the five miles to Gartmore along a 'parish-road' leading over a moor 'where no sound was heard but the shrill whistle of the plovey [plover] and occasionally the unearthly hum of some butto [*possibly buteo – buzzard*] on the wing'. By now it was dark with a 'half-full moon'. It was difficult to get somewhere to stay for the night but eventually he found a bed which was 'at least clean if in a poor garrett'. Here supper consisted of a crust of bread, cheese and a glass of porter. After a good night's sleep Jones walked on to the village of Aberfoyle for breakfast, through exceedingly beautiful scenery with views across the Lake of Mentieth as far as Stirling. Breakfast at an inn was followed by a visit to Loch Ard, two miles distant, 'the most picturesque and beautiful of all the lakes I have

3.4: Professors Court, Glasgow University, before 1870. (University of Glasgow Archive Service, University Photographic Collection GB0248 PHU38/2)

yet seen. As a subject for the painter it is everything that one could desire'. He returned to the inn, then headed north over the hill into the Trossachs.

Jones's encounter with this magnificent landscape led him to reflect not only on its beauty but also on how it might have been experienced in the past by Scots in the search for liberty:

> After toiling up the steep ascent came upon a waterfall of no small pretensions to beauty. The wild heath and rocky hills by which it is encircled renders it just such a place as a Covenanter of old would have chosen as his hiding place, or a stream in which while fleeing from his pursuer the outcast for conscience sake might lean to quench his thirst. We could not resist the temptation of bathing our heated hands in the rolling torrent and with forehead bare drew in a copious draft of its sweet waters. Full many a persecuted [. . .] may have done that before, but he could not have done so with a lowly spirit here in the wide [. . .]. Moor and mountain spoke of liberty. The heron and the lark soaring aloft spoke of freedom, and the babbling brook bounding from rock to rock raises a joyous hymn of praise to liberty. Who then would be a slave in body or in mind?

Jones then entered a 'terrifically grand' scene. Having gained the summit, and leaving the path, 'the most splendid views we ever witnessed breaks upon us – Loch Venacher, L. Achray & L. Katrine lay before us, the first complete, the other(s) only thro' a gap in the wild Trossachs'. At the bottom of the mountain a farmhouse provided refreshment in the form of Highland hospitality, with plenty of bread, cheese and milk. The way along the shore of Loch Achray took him to the Bridge of Turk and the banks of Loch Katrine, before he arrived at his lodgings at Stewarts Inn at Ardcheanochrochan in time for tea. A climb up the hill behind the inn gave him wet feet, which he dried in the kitchen. Later that evening, over a tumbler of warm toddy, he wrote about his experiences here, concluding that 'the gorgeous picture of the Trossachs and L. Kateran drawn by Sir W. Scott falls very far short of the reality'.[34] The Trossachs were already popular with tourists. Thirty years before Jones's visit James Hogg, the 'Ettrick Shepherd', wrote an account of visiting Loch Katrine and the Bridge of Turk, saying that knowledge of the *Lady of the Lake* was essential if the wonders of the landscape were to be enjoyed to the full. Interestingly he comments that 'About one o'clock, I reached Mr Stuarts the guide's house, the name of which I never can either pronounce or spell …': perhaps like Jones he found himself at Stewarts Inn at Ardcheanochrochan, seemingly a difficult word even for a Scot, albeit one from the Borders.[35]

Ten days later Arthur Jones left Glasgow and his studies for good and travelled south to Northampton. However, before we follow that stage of his story we must return to the summer of 1839, when Arthur Jones made what seems to be his first contact with the county of Somerset.

Chapter Four

First Contacts with Somerset

A T THE END OF HIS FIRST YEAR IN GLASGOW, in the summer of 1839, Jones returned to Bridgend where he spent more time exploring the area and collecting geological specimens. He also took on a temporary appointment at the Free Christian and Unitarian chapel in Crewkerne in south Somerset, a time which was to have significant implications for both his personal and professional life. In the absence of evidence to the contrary it seems probable that it was the invitation to Crewkerne that provided his first contact with Somerset and, as nationally the Unitarian/Dissenting community was small and closely connected, his name might well have been obtained through the Dr Williams Trust.

Crewkerne is a small market town, largely built of the warm yellow oolitic limestone that characterises many of the towns and villages of the area. In 1841 it was home to 4414 people and, in addition to serving the surrounding area, had an important manufacturing role, with weaving and the production of sail cloth being particularly important. The Free Christian and Unitarian chapel is a small attractive limestone and slate building in Hermitage Street, a few hundred yards to the south of the town centre. Founded in 1733, it had by the 1830s a small congregation drawn from the town and nearby villages. The chapel accounts record that in 1839 the sum of £7 7s. was paid to

4.1: The Unitarian and Free Christian Chapel, Hermitage Street, Crewkerne. (AC)

the 'Rev. W.A. Jones' (although still only a student he was given a title) for his time serving the congregation, while John Munford, who lived with his wife Prudence in Market Square, received rather more than this, £9 9s, for 'nine weeks board of W.A. Jones'.[36]

Among the congregation at the chapel were members of the Blake family, notable Dissenters in the county whose antecedents included Admiral Robert Blake of Cromwell's time. The Blakes were nominally Presbyterians until 1813 when it became a legal option for non-conformists to adopt publicly the Unitarian label. The family home in the town was an elegant double fronted house on Market Street where today a Blue Plaque commemorates their occupation. Succeeding his father William who died in 1799, the Revd William Blake had been the minister at the chapel until his death in 1821, and Jones developed a lifelong friendship with his son, yet another William who was only three years his senior. Jones's time in the town seems to have come at a difficult period for the chapel, as after the Revd William Blake's death the congregation was looked after briefly by the Revd William Wilson, who was followed in turn by the Revd Sam Walker until March 1839. A series of visiting ministers then served the chapel, of which Jones was one, until the appointment of the Revd John Teggin in 1840.

The story of the Blakes of South Petherton has already been told, but despite Jones's close ties with them there is surprisingly little said about him in that account.[37] There is one specific reference, to the marriage of William Blake's son William Farewell to Arthur Jones's daughter Ellen in 1882: '(her) father was a Welshman who eventually became a Unitarian minister in Taunton. He had married Margaret Blake, William Blake's sister'. Not much is said about the interests, especially geology, that Blake and Jones shared. This common interest in geology must have become apparent soon after they met. In a letter to Blake in October 1839, written in Bridgend before he returned to Glasgow for his second year, Jones promised to send fossils that he had collected from quarries around Bridgend, at Oxillan, Coity, Merthyrmawr and St Brides. The local Lias limestone had proved to be a particularly rich source and the collection included ammonites, belemnites, nautili and a pentacrinite. The samples were sent by sea, via Porthcawl and Bridgwater.[38]

It may be that Blake had no particular expertise in scientific matters, a view taken by the writer of his obituary in the *Proceedings* of the Somerset Archaeological and Natural History Society in 1901, at least with reference to archaeology:

> Although we are unable to record him as an authority on matters archaeological, yet he always had a great respect for them, and was ever ready to join in furthering the interests of our Society to the best of his power, from the date of its inauguration until his death.[39]

While there is no mention of geology in this quotation it is clear that Blake was keenly interested in the subject. On 11 November 1836 his sister Margaret wrote to him at Brenley in Kent, their mother's family home: 'I walk every day if I can and always look for fossils for you but have not found any worth keeping; have you found any; I intend some day to go to the quarry by Bincombe before you come home'.[40] Bincombe Hill overlooks the centre of Crewkerne from the north, rising to 347ft. It is now a public park and the quarry on the north side of the hill has in recent times been overtaken by development. Such quarries often provided opportunities for local people to explore the geology of their area, and forty five years after Margaret Blake's visit the geologist Horace B. Woodward described the site thus in the *Proceedings* of the Somerset Archaeological and Natural History Society:

At Mr Lye's brickyard at Crewkerne, the Fuller's Earth clays are worked for making bricks, tiles and drain pipes, and here the beds are seen resting on the Inferior Oolite, and faulted against the Midford Sands. Thus a useful assemblage of strata is met with in one series of openings, the sand being serviceable to the brick-makers, and the lime being burnt for mortar. It will be noticed, too, that the Inferior Oolite limestone occurs in more solid blocks beneath the clay covering than it does when exposed to the influence of the atmosphere. A few fossils may be obtained from the clay, such as *Belemnites parallelus, Ostrea acummiata, Waldheima ornithocephala, and Rhynchonella various.*[41]

In the spring of 1841 Blake visited Lyme Regis where he met Mary Anning and inspected some of her fossil specimens which were for sale. Following his visit she wrote to him on 17 March:

> Agreable to my promise I write to inform you that I have now by me a small Ichthyosaurus (near the size of the one you saw when at Lyme) price £5, also a head sternum paddle with cervical vertebrae of another price £2, and a large headed jaw also a scapula carrcoid and humeris of a plesio with a number of other second rate specimens, if you Sir would like to ride over and look at them; with best and grateful thanks for yr kindness when at Lyme.[42]

From 1843 onwards Blake kept a notebook of lists of geological specimens, starting with several collected in the Mont Blanc area and including also a list of Pyrenees specimens sent to him by Margaret, Jones's eldest daughter. [43]

4.2: William Blake. (Blake Archives (BA))

Chapter Five
Northampton

ARTHUR JONES GRADUATED FROM GLASGOW UNIVERSITY in the spring of 1841. The university's early records do not include the class of a degree, but as he studied for three years rather than four it would have been an Ordinary MA, not Honours; Scottish universities gave MAs rather than the BAs offered in England. However just before his graduation Jones told William Blake that he would be receiving an 'honorable ' MA and a record of students at the Carmarthen College published in 1901 states that he received an honourable distinction in classics. [44]

Glasgow as a city had not appealed to the young man from rural Wales who seems to have been much happier in the surrounding countryside. Shortly before finishing his studies in 1841 Jones wrote to William Blake in Crewkerne, describing his feelings about his studies and his future. It was clear that he had had enough of the academic life: 'I assure you that it is a blessed release to have all the hindrance of <u>nine examinations</u> removed from one's shoulders'. He was also sorry to inform his friend that 'I have become a very desultory reader, having thrown aside my Aristotle and my Mathematics, my Sophocles and my Tacitus but I must not allow myself to revel too much in the sweets of light literature', a rare hint that this serious young man did occasionally indulge in the

5.1: The centre of Northampton as Arthur Jones would have known it. (Extract from a map of 1843 by W.W. Laws (Northamptonshire Record Office))

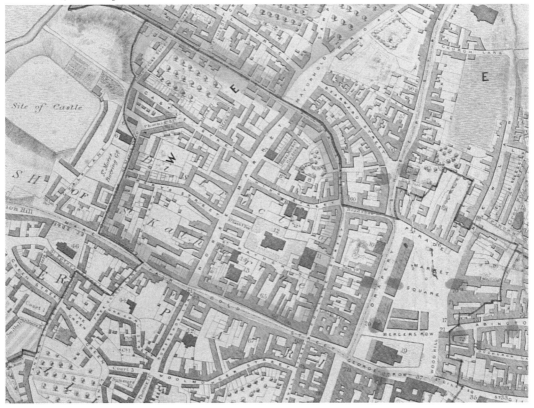

lighter things of life, although he felt obliged to return to serious work before long and intended to spend a few days improving his knowledge of geology. Turning to his future he said that he longed to escape from the 'smoky and dirty city' and could be happy to spend years in a 'small retired town or village'. Perhaps he was thinking of Carmarthen or of Crewkerne and his friends there. He also felt that men were 'morally' better in the country than in towns, but added that he would have to go where duty called. [45]

Jones's aspirations for his future were not satisfied, initially at least, for 'duty' called him not to a 'small retired town or village' but to the market and industrial town of Northampton, where he had been appointed to the post of minister of the Unitarian chapel in King Street and was to be paid £25 per quarter. In the early nineteenth century Northampton was growing rapidly, its population of 7,020 inhabitants in 1801 increasing to 15,351 by 1831. The next ten years saw a further growth in population of 5,879 – almost 40% - so Jones came to a town of over 21,000 people. The town had a variety of industries but the main one, in which a third of men were employed, was shoe-making, at that time an un-mechanised home-based activity. In recent years the town had started expanding beyond the limits of the former town walls and had seen, since 1830, the establishment of a range of public institutions and facilities.[46] These included the Water Works Company engine house and reservoir (1836); the Northamptonshire Union Bank (1836); the Union Work House (1836); St. Thomas' hospital (founded in about.1450, building erected 1833); the Lunatic Asylum (1836); the Cemetery (1846) and the New Borough Gaol (1846). There were also, which would have been of great interest to Jones, a Mechanics' Institute, a Religious and Useful Knowledge Society and the remains of a medieval castle (no longer there as it was levelled to make way for a railway station at some time after 1861).[47]

Arthur Jones's ministry in Northampton formally started in April 1841 but he could not escape from Glasgow until the 28th of the month, because it was on that day that he experienced 'the highest consumation of collegeate ambition' when 'John Knox's greasy old cap is placed on our heads and we rise honorable MA'. [47] He left Glasgow on 6 May, and travelled to the port of Ardrossan, on the Ayrshire coast, by the railway opened the previous year. Here he took the coastal vessel *Fire King* to Fleetwood, in Lancashire, arriving there after a rough journey at 8.15 the following morning. It seems that he was a good sailor as he 'slept very comfortably though the vessel rolled and tossed about very much'. From Fleetwood, in 1841 a relatively new port and town, he travelled by train firstly to Preston, with a First Class seat, and then from Birmingham to Blisworth, in a Second Class carriage because First Class was not available. As the railway did not reach Northampton itself until 1845 he had to drive the four miles into the town – presumably by a local coach or carrier which met the train.

He took the pulpit in Northampton for the first time on the second Sunday in May, shortly after his 23rd birthday. The chapel had been founded in 1827 as a break-away congregation from the Castle Hill chapel and he was the third minister, following Noah Jones and J.C. Meeke. All three ministries were successful and the congregation and the Unitarian approach were doing well.[48] The congregation was fully involved in civic activities and had a strong liberal tradition. Information about Jones's ministry in Northampton at this time is unfortunately limited but it does appear, as we shall see, that his ministry was not always straightforward and his personal life was marked by tragedy. However, for his interests in natural history and archaeology his time in the town was very important. At first he lodged in Gold Street with George Baker and his sister Anne, both members of his congregation, later moving to a house in Spencer Parade opposite the hospital. George Baker (1781-1851) was an important historian of Northamptonshire, being author of *The History and Antiquities of the County of Northampton*, published in five parts between 1822 and 1841. Anne Baker (1786-1861) assisted her brother with his work, compiling the sections on geology and botany for his History, but was also a notable author in her own right. In 1854 she published her *Glossary of Northamptonshire Words and Phrases – with Examples of their Colloquial Use and Illustrations from Various Authors; to which are added the Customs of the County.*[49]

It was this contact with the Bakers that furthered Jones's interest in antiquarian matters, not only George's work but also Anne's interest in geology, botany and dialect; Jones is in the list of subscribers to Anne's dialect book. It was also through George Baker that Jones met the antiquary Sir Thomas Phillips, who purchased many of Baker's papers when the latter gave up his antiquarian work in the 1840s because of ill-health. In July 1845 Arthur and George visited Carmarthen and had proposed to call on Phillips at his home in Broadway in the Cotswolds on the way home, but did not do so because they were delayed in Wales.[50]

A major change in Arthur's life came after a year in Northampton when he entered the state of matrimony, but his bride was not from the town but came from south Somerset. Mary Cuff was the daughter of James Cuff and his wife Joanna (née Fitchett) of Merriott, a village two miles to the north of Crewkerne. James and Joanna were married by licence on 13 August 1799 in the parish church at Nynehead near Wellington in Somerset. Joanna Fitchett does not appear in the Nynehead baptism register and it is possible that she was employed at Nynehead Court, the home since about 1590 of the Sanford family. In the 1850s Jones was to become a friend of William Ayshford Sanford and a frequent visitor to the Court. The Cuff family lived at a house on Ashwell Lane in the southern part of Merriott, close to the parish boundary with Crewkerne. The tithe survey for Merriott in December 1842 shows William Fitchett Cuff, James and Joanna's only surviving son, as the owner/occupier of a house on the south side of the village.

5.2: The Cuff family tomb, Merriott church, near Crewkerne. (AC)

He also owned about 88 acres of land in the parish, three cottages and 901 acres in Crewkerne, all but 114 acres let out. Presumably he inherited the Merriott property on the death of his father, as his older brother, John, had died in 1833. Judging by the size of the Cuff tomb in Merriott churchyard and the amount of land they owned the family must have been of some significance in the village.

Mary Cuff was born on 11 December 1808, the youngest of five children, and was baptised at the Crewkerne chapel by the minister Dr William Blake. The Cuffs were members of the chapel and regular subscribers to its funds, so Mary and Arthur must have met when he did 'supply' there in the summer of 1839. She clearly made an impression on him despite, or perhaps because of, the fact that she was nine and a half years older than him! Writing to William Blake on 15 November 1839 Jones sent 'Kind remembrances . . . also to Miss Mary Cuff if still at Taunton',[51] and the entry in his Glasgow diary for 11 December in that year reads 'Dined. After dinner took a glass of toddy to celebrate the birth-day of a particular friend'. He believed that Mary shared his interests and would have been of the same mind about hunting, one matter on which he disagreed with William Blake:

> Though I am sympathetic with you in most things, in that I confess I fail. It were out of place in me even if I could; a hunting Unitarian parson would indeed be a phenomenon. Besides I am too much of a cowperite. What does Miss Mary say as to the propriety of hunting down the poor hare? Her views are probably similar to my own.[52]

Arthur and Mary were married in the chapel at Crewkerne on 9 June 1842 by the Revd John Teggin. Mary's mother had died on 17 August 1841 aged 70 and her father seven months later on 25 March aged 78, so it seems likely that as the youngest unmarried daughter she had been looking after them and was therefore not free to marry. There is evidence that the Cuffs' life at this time was not an easy one. In 1841 Margaret Blake wrote to her brother William: 'I am quite grieved about the poor Cuffs, they seem to be so very uncomfortable. I fear they do not some how manage or do as they ought – they are always in trouble'.[53]

Sadly Arthur and Mary's marriage came to an untimely end after only four months: Mary died at about 2 p.m. on 26 October in the same year at the age of 33, of 'anaemia from repeated uterine haemorrages', possibly a miscarriage.[54] She was buried in the Cuff family tomb in Merriott churchyard, a table tomb of Ham stone standing on the left of the path to the south porch. The notice in the *Northampton Mercury* read 'On the 26 inst. Mary the beloved wife of the Rev. W.A. Jones of this town, Unitarian minister. In life she was pure, patient and loving, in death calm, peaceful and resigned'. Writing to the Blake family the day after Mary's death Jones said that he felt sorely the loss of his wife: 'It has pleased him in whose hands are the destinies of Man to take unto himself the object of my devoted love and leave me thus lonely and dejected to mourn her loss'.[55] During the following twelve months he took a break from his duties at the chapel and reassessed his future as a Unitarian minister.

A European journey, 1843

Early in 1843 Jones resolved to take time away from his ministry in Northampton. In a letter to the Blakes on 27 January he wrote:

. . . you will be glad to hear that my health and spirits are much better than they have been. At the same time they are both far from what I could wish them to be. I trust a little change of scene in the spring may effect what time does not. At one time I felt much inclined to renew the student life. I am now wavering, or rather inclined to continue a laborer in the vineyard. I do not know what might be the affects of so great a change in my mode of life, and I should indeed regret ever to lose any portion of the attachment I feel for the duties of the Christian Ministry. Besides this, I am so attached to my little flock, and have experienced so much sympathy and kindness at their hands, that the thought of leaving them becomes truly painful. In the course of a month or two I shall have framed some more definite plans than I have at present. And about that time it is not unlikely we may meet in Somerset. I have promised to pay a visit to my friends in Merriott some time in March.[56]

It is not known if he did go to Merriott, but at the end of the month he set off on an excursion of 1,100 miles through northern Europe. Quite why he chose that area is not known but on his return from these travels he wrote on 20 July to William Blake, who was proposing a similar journey later that year:

I am glad to hear you propose to yourself an excursion on the Continent. I am sure it will do you a world of good in all respects and afford you not only pleasure and gratification for the moment but supply you with very many pleasing reminiscences to dwell upon. I wish you could have accompanied me, I am sure you would have approved of the route.[57]

At the end of March 1843 Jones travelled up to London, his first task being to obtain a passport. The copy of his passport held in the Somerset Archives is a revealing document for two reasons, firstly how he obtained the document and, secondly, what it says about him.[58] The first is more surprising in that it was issued not by the British Government but by M.H. Castellain in the name of the King of the Belgians. It seems that at that time to obtain a British passport required substantial funds and a contact with someone of influence. The Belgian authorities, perhaps as Belgium was a relatively new country having been founded only in 1830, were it seems less demanding. In fact the document appears, in today's terms, to be a cross between a passport and a visa. Issued on 24 March, valid for one year and headed No.1 (was it the first one issued by the Belgian consul or the first of that year?) the document gives Jones the authority to travel in the following words (in translation from the French):

We Consul in London of His Majesty the King of the Belgians entreat the Civil and Military Authorities charged with the interior Police of the Kingdom and of all the Countries friends and allies of Belgium to allow free passage to Mr. William Arthur Jones, minister, native of South Wales and resident of Northampton.

Going from London to Belgium via Antwerp for a pleasure trip and to give him help and protection in case of need.

The second interesting point is that Jones's European journey took place long before a passport could be accompanied by a photograph of the holder. Instead there is a written description of his appearance, from which we learn that the 24 year old William Arthur Jones was 5' 8" in height, with blue eyes, an aquiline nose, an average forehead and mouth, a round chin and an oval face. Thus today he would be short in stature but would have been average or even tall for the middle of the nineteenth century.

His route through northern Europe can be ascertained in part from the signed 'authorities to travel' that were issued to him, presumably by Belgian consuls in the cities and towns he visited. As this was in the days before the existence of a unified German state Jones had to pass through several member states of the German Confederation

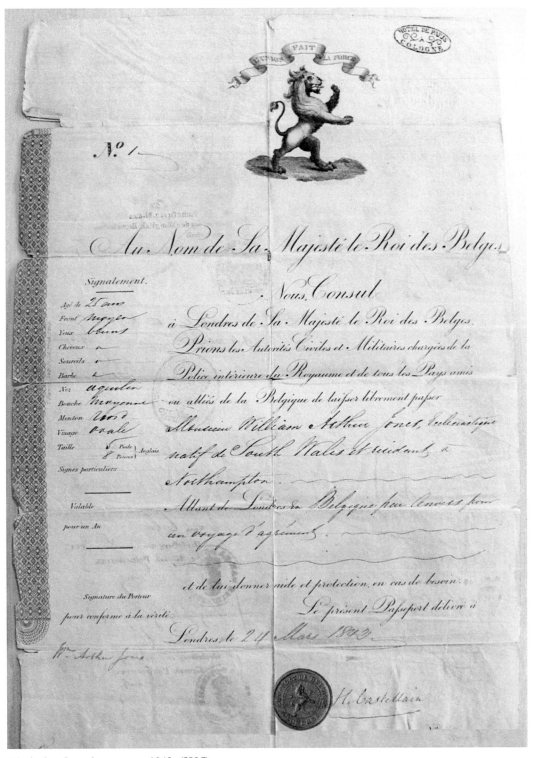

5.3: Arthur Jones's passport, 1843. (SHC)

5.4: The Rhine at Cologne, 1847 from a watercolour by artist Anne Wilson, taken from *A European Journey - Two Sisters Abroad* by Mary Wilson, edited by Jennifer Simpson. (Reproduced with permission of Bloomsbury Publishing PLC)

that had been set up by the Treaty of Versailles in 1815. Unfortunately he provides few details of what he looked at on is journey but nevertheless it is worth quoting in full his own account as relayed to William Blake.[59] It should be noted that the names of places he visited are sometimes not the modern ones, either by virtue of changed spelling or because they have been replaced, such of those now in the Czech Republic.[60]

I think it embraces almost all objects of greatest interest in Northern Germany, and as you propose going thither so soon I will just give you an outline of the route. I left London by steampacket of course and landed at Antwerp. Brussels, Mechlin, Liege, Aix-la-Chapelle are on the railroad to Cologne and all well worth visiting as you are aware. The Rhine becomes interesting a few miles above Cologne and the steampackets of which these four or five in the day stop at all the objects of interest to land and take up passengers. From Cologne I went to Bonn where I stayed some days and then met with my friend Sadler who afterwards was my companion. I gave my portmanteau and hat case to the Prussian govt. authorities to convey to Heidelberg and reserved only what was absolutely necessary for change in my Knapsack, a very tidy affair sold at Bonn for about 8/-. From Bonn by steamer to the foot of the Drakenfels. At the hotel on the Drakenfels we slept, and the next morning having crossed the river before breakfast we walked along the banks of the Rhine to Remagau, where we branched off over the mountains to the Vale of Ahr, reaching Ahrweiler very easily the same day. The next day walked to Altenhar which is the a (sic) small town in the midst of the wildest scenery I have seen in the Rhine district. From Altenhar we walked over the mountains by the Lake of Laach to Andernach where we took a steamer to Coblentz. From Coblentz to Bingen is three days walk, and includes the finest and most romantic portion of the Rhine. Those who are pressed for time may take the

5.5: Heidelberg Castle, 1847 from a watercolour by artist Anne Wilson, taken from *A European Journey - Two Sisters Abroad* by Mary Wilson, edited by Jennifer Simpson. (Reproduced with permission of Bloomsbury Publishing PLC)

> steamer and land at Boppart and St Goar, but it is only by walking that the beauties are thoroughly to be seen and enjoyed. From Bingen we went to Mayence by steamer – thence by railroad to Wiesbaden and Franckfort. The best way thence to Heidelberg is by Darmstadt along the famous Bergstrasse. Heidelberg never disappoints any one however high their expectations may have been. From thence you have rail to Manheim, rail within 3 or 4 miles of Schwetzingen – the German Versailles – rail to Carlsrhue, which is not far from Baden Baden, steamer to Strasburg rail thence to Basle, and then you are in Switzerland. From Strasburg there is a direct communication to Paris.[61]

Jones's companion was probably Thomas Sadler, four years his junior, who was studying at Bonn. After taking a PhD at Erlangen University, Nuremberg, in 1844 he became the Unitarian minister in Hampstead in 1846 and was a noted author on religious matters. He later joined the Somerset Archaeological and Natural History Society and the Bath and West of England Society.

At Heidelberg Jones left the valley of the Rhine and headed east into Bavaria. He now writes in the first person so it might reasonably be assumed that Thomas Sadler ended his part of the journey here and travelled back to Bonn.

> I have not been higher up on the Rhine than Manheim. From Heidelberg I took the steamer up the Neckar to Mosbach or rather Neckarelz, whence a diligence conveys passengers to Wurtzburg, thence I went to Nuremberg, Carlsbad, Prague, Teplitz, came down upon the Elbe at Tetschen, walked thro' the Saxon Switzerland, which I am sure would interest you as a geologist not less than as a lover of the grand and picturesque in scenery. There are steamers on the Elbe almost from Prague to Dresden and thence

to the mouth of the Elbe. But once at Dresden you have railroads to every place of interest.

At Dresden I bad adieu to the beautiful in scenery. The country is dull, flat, and uninteresting, and fortunately you have [a] railway to Leipzig, Halle, Wittemberg, Berlin, Potsdam, and back again to Magdeburg, then a steampacket down the Elbe to Hamburg. These were the places I visited. Until I left Heidelberg I found English spoken at all the chief hotels. From thence until I came to Dresden little or none. French does every where at hotels – a little German is necessary in Bavaria and Bohemia.

If you go up the Rhine and through Belgium, you should by all means get Murray's Handbook for Northern Germany, it's by far the best guide book, and if you read 'Germany' by Dr Bisset Hawkins you will profit more by your visit. There are things I have myself learnt. I wish I had known them before I left England for the Continent.

When you get to Cologne I would likewise advise you to purchase a map or Panorama of the Rhine from Mayence to Cologne. There are two published, the best for about 9/- or 3 thalers prussain which is well worth the money. If I were not so far I would lend you mine. But this we may talk of when I know more of your plans.

This letter to William Blake shows that in the three months of his journey Jones had used almost every form of transport then available:

Route	Method of travel
London-Antwerp	Steam packet
Antwerp-Mechelen-Brussels-Liege Aix-la-Chapelle-(Aachen)-Cologne	Train
Cologne-Bonn-Drakenfels (castle)	River steamer on Rhine
Drakenfels-Remagau	Foot along river
Remagau-Ahrweiler-Altenhar-Lake of Laach-Andernach	Foot
Andermach-Coblentz	River steamer
Coblentze-Bingen	Foot (3 days)
Bingen-Mayence(Mainz)	River steamer
Mayence-Weisbaden-Franckfort	Train
Franckfort-Darmstadt-Heidelberg	Foot(?)
Heidelberg-Neckarelz	River steamer
Neckarelz-Wurtzberg	Diligence (a form of stage coach)
Wurtzberg-Nuremburg-Carlsbad-Prague-Teplitz-Tetschen	Train
Lower Saxony-Dresden	Foot
Dresden-Leipzig-Halle-Wittemberg-Berlin-Potsdam- Magdeburg	Train
Magdeburg-Hamburg	Steam packet
Hamburg-London	Steam packet

As Jones had told the Blakes in January, the idea of leaving the Unitarian ministry to study theology was already in his mind as a possibility, but by the end of his tour he was giving it more serious thought and was considering pursuing his studies in Geneva. Since the sixteenth century the Swiss town had been a centre for Protestantism and Jones had written to his friend and mentor Dr James Yates for advice on how to proceed. Yates

5.6: Map of Arthur Jones's European tour in 1843. (Ian Coleby)

wrote to him on 4 August 1843, noting that his health had improved 'and that you have had so pleasant, improving and successful journey. I also take a very great interest in your plan of further study and am very desirous of giving you the best advice I can upon the subject'.[62] The letter goes on with advice especially on what was involved in becoming a student of theology in the Academy of Geneva. Jones's letter to William Blake shows that on his return to Northampton a move to Geneva was still a serious proposition:

> As soon as I hear more of Geneva I will let you know. My friends here have done all they can to prevail upon me to withdraw my resignation, but that cannot be. The more I think of the step I am about to take the more convinced I am of the [desirability?] of it on my account.
> Hoping they might prevail upon me to change my intentions my congregation have hitherto taken no steps towards securing the services of a successor. However I hope to be able to leave before the end of September, I fear not before that.

He had already decided to travel to Geneva via Paris, staying there some weeks if time permitted, and had letters of introduction from James Yates to his friends in the Swiss town. What led him to change his mind is not clear but it might have been pressure from his Northampton congregation. He had resigned from his post, but no steps had been taken to replace him, and on 1 July 1843 a resolution was passed imploring him to stay:

> At a 'publick' meeting held in the Unitarian Chapel Northampton on Sunday July the 1st 1843 Mr. Thos. Sharp in the chair. Resolved unanimously that we have heard the announcement of the intended resignation of our highly respected Minister Mr. Jones with feelings of the deepest regret, and that no steps be taken towards providing a successor till after we have had the opportunity of personal communication with him.[63]

Jones stayed in Northampton where his interests extended beyond the chapel, as he said in a letter to the Revd Jerome Murch of Bath on 5 January 1845: 'I am on the committee of almost every public institution in the town'.[64] However, it seems that he was still not settled and his correspondence with the congregation at the time of his move from the town in 1849 suggests that he was having difficulties with some members of his congregation. He was also keen to be in Somerset, probably to be closer to the Blakes, not only William but also his sister Margaret whose name is often mentioned in Jones's letters. On one occasion, knowing that she was interested in curiosities, he sent her a leaf of ivy from the 'Brig o'Doone'.[65] He accepted an invitation to preach at the Unitarian Chapel in Bath on 15 January, with a view to taking up a post there. Whether he was turned down or the post did not suit him is not known but he did comment on the appointments system, saying he was not in favour of the competitive approach.[66] However, the visit might also have brought him another Somerset contact in the form of the geologist Charles Moore, who was a member of the Bath congregation.

Although the move to Bath did not happen, Jones's links with the Blake family remained strong and on 1 January 1846, now aged 28, he married Margaret Blake (eight months his junior) at the Mary Street Chapel in Taunton. Three years later he finally moved with his family, Margaret and their son Downing Blake Jones (born in October 1846), south from Northampton to Somerset where he took up the post of minister of the Christ Church chapel at Bridgwater. The testimonies given by his Northampton congregation included a letter on behalf of the Sunday School which showed that there had been problems: 'We know that we have not been as attentive as we ought to have been and we feel sorry for the pain we have caused you by our misconduct and sincerely ask your forgiveness and it is our earnest prayer that the God and Father of our Lord Jesus Christ be with you to bless and prosper you', but generally they were full of praise and it is clear that overall he had been a well-regarded minister at the King Street chapel.[67] His move to Bridgwater was accompanied by a letter from a fellow Unitarian minister, John Kentish of Park Vale in Edgbaston, Birmingham:

> You and Mrs Jones, I presume, will be travelling during a part of next week. I heartily wish you a safe and comfortable journey, good weather and a happy interview with your beloved relations.
> I can scarcely conceive of any thing, of the kind, more agreeable and welcome than the meetings of yourselves (together with your children) with your mother, and with Mrs J's kindred in Somersetshire.[68]

Chapter Six
Somerset
Bridgwater

IN THE YEARS before the Jones family moved to Bridgwater the town had grown considerably, reaching a population of 10450 in 1841, almost 7000 more than in 1801. Its position on the tidal part of the River Parrett, a few miles from the Bristol Channel, was an important factor in its development as a significant trading centre in medieval times. As a port it had important links not only

6.1: The south side of King Square, Bridgwater, 1865. No 3 is in the middle of the terrace. (Blake Museum, Bridgwater)

across the channel to South Wales but also to the continent, especially the Bordeaux region some of whose wine found its way into England through Bridgwater. By the nine-

6.3: The older children of Arthur and Margaret Jones, taken before 1864; from top – Downing, Margaret, Sarah, William Arthur. (BA)

6.2: Margaret Jones née Blake – Arthur Jones's second wife. (BA)

6.4: Mary Jones – a photograph taken in Montpellier in 1867-68. (BA)

teenth century it had become a centre for brick and tile making, products used in many of the buildings of the town and the surrounding area. The Jones family moved into a house at 3 King's Square, which together with the adjoining Castle Street forms the architecturally most interesting part of the town. The elegant red brick three storey houses on two sides of the Square (it was not completed) were built at the end of the eighteenth cen-

6.5: Dampiet Street, Bridgwater, 1865 (Blake Museum, Bridgwater)

tury. By 1851 Arthur and Margaret had three children, Downing Blake (aged 4) and two daughters who were born in Bridgwater - Margaret and Sarah Elizabeth (aged 2 and 1). The family must have been quite well-off as they had three live-in servants, 24 year-old Elizabeth Brewer (born in Cannington just to the north west of the town), Harriet Wallis (aged 32) and Lucy Wallis (aged 23). Harriet and Lucy were born in Peterborough and Grantham respectively, suggesting that they could have come to Bridgwater with the Jones family. The neighbours were corn merchant John Payne at no. 2 and John Farquhar, a merchant, at no. 4.[69]

Jones took up his post at the Christ Church chapel in Dampiet Street, close to the town centre, at Michaelmas in 1849. Bridgwater had a long tradition of religious dissent,

6.6: The doorway of Christchurch Chapel, Bridgwater. (AC)

the chapel having been first licensed for worship by Dissenters in the Presbyterian tradition in 1689. Made of red brick it was rebuilt, probably in 1788, incorporating a shell-hood door of 1688 and with a Dutch gabled pediment and a Venetian window. During the eighteenth century the congregation became increasingly Unitarian in sentiment, from 1809 meetings of the Western Unitarian Society were held at Bridgwater, and in 1815 the congregation was avowedly Unitarian.

In addition to his ministerial duties, Jones attended meetings of the town's Literary and Scientific Institution; this had been founded in about 1838 and put on lectures on a variety of subjects. It seems that Jones did not have a central role in the Institution as the Annual General Meeting in 1850 was the first one he had attended for some time, but he was moved to propose a resolution of the future of the organisation. In fact at this time press reports suggest that it was not doing too well.[70] Attendances were low and there was a problem of inexperienced speakers. A meeting in August 1852 held to revive the institution stimulated an editorial in the *Somerset County Gazette* on 28 August 1852 but by then Jones had moved to take up the position of minister at the Mary Street Chapel in Taunton.

Taunton

The town of Taunton stands at a crossing of the River Tone between the Blackdown and Quantock Hills. To the east lie the Somerset Levels while to the west is the upper part of the agriculturally rich Vale of Taunton Deane. From the early Middle Ages it was the centre of a vast estate owned by the Bishop of Winchester, with its own castle next to the river crossing. In the nineteenth century the town grew rapidly, from a population of 5794 in 1801 it had reached 13,119 in 1851 and was to grow even more as the century passed. This expansion had seen a concentration on silk manufacture and better communications via the Tone navigation, turnpike roads and, in 1842, the coming of Brunel's railway. Urban improvements included fine terraces of houses, such as the

6.7: Arrival of the mail coach at Taunton. Edward Turle, *c.*1840 (SANHS)

Crescent, built to serve the gentry and affluent middle classes.[71]

In the town's religious life the nonconformist traditions were particularly strong, in contrast with the Established Church which in the eighteenth century was in the doldrums. The various denominations were building their own chapels. A Baptist chapel had been established on Mary Street, close to the town centre, by 1691 and was rebuilt in 1721. Movement of a congregation from one tradition to another was not uncommon and by the time Arthur Jones arrived in Taunton in 1852 this chapel was clearly in the Unitarian tradition. Jones took over from the Revd Robert Montgomery who had been at the chapel since 1835 and who had left a flourishing congregation. The census of religious activity taken in 1851, for which the return for the chapel was made by Mr Montgomery, showed that on Sunday 30 March the attendance at both the morning and evening services was 150 and that there were 70 'Sunday scholars' in the morning and 80 in the afternoon. A year later at the chapel's General Annual Meeting on 11 April 1852 Mr Montgomery gave a fairly encouraging report of the life of the congregation, although he had some reservations:

> Mr Montgomery dwelt strongly on the neglect and apathy of the congregation in allowing the Boys Sunday School to sink for want of teachers, intimating that this was probably the last occasion on which they would hear comments from him on that subject. He stated that the Girls' School on the other hand was well supported by the energy of the Ladies, that the Provident and Blanket Societies, the Libraries, the benefit club and other institutions were flourishing and that (with the exception above alluded to) the Congregation generally was in a satisfactory condition.[72]

This was indeed the last occasion on which Mr Montgomery reviewed the well-being of the chapel, as on 4 May the trustees noted the receipt of his resignation as minister and agreed to make enquiries about the availability of 'disengaged ministers', presumably those not in post elsewhere. In fact only three weeks later it was agreed to invite Jones to become the minister, at a salary of £180 per annum (£30 more than his predecessor). His appointment is not surprising as Jones was well known to some members of the congregation; William Blake was one of them, having lived at Bishops Hull on the edge of Taunton since his marriage in 1844, and Arthur's wife Margaret would have welcomed

6.8: The original façade of the Mary Street chapel, Taunton. (SHC)

6.9: The Mary Street chapel today. The façade was added after Jones's time. (AC)

the opportunity to be closer to her brother.

Life at the chapel under Jones's ministry continued as under his predecessor, with continual improvements to the buildings and occasional difficulties. In 1855 the chapel's Moore's Charity had distributed £10 2s 6d among 60 poor persons belonging to the congregation but at that time there were concerns about the falling income from members, a situation remedied by stern words from the pulpit. Jones was an active and well-liked minister but his own beliefs did from time to time raise eyebrows in the town, a matter that will be addressed in a later chapter. On 29 April 1860 he gave his report on the state and prospects of the chapel's institutions, which were in his view satisfactory, although he also commented on 'the various changes which had taken place in the congregation during the past year, looking forward gloomily to the future'. This might have been a reflection

6.10: Silver Street House, Taunton. Jones's home from 1852-1866. The facade was added later (AC)

6.11: Silver Street House from the rear, showing the original brickwork. (AC)

of the difficulties in his family life. After moving from Bridgwater the family continued to grow, with the addition of three sons and two daughters, but his wife Margaret was now seriously ill and, with the hope of an improvement in her condition, he took her to Dawlish in south Devon in May 1860. Served by Brunel's South Devon railway from Exeter, the resort had risen 'from a mere fishing village to the dignity of a fashionable watering place' and had become 'one of the prettiest places along the coast to pass a quiet summer month', despite the coast being marred by the very railway that had encouraged its development.[73] The couple stayed at 9 Strand where handsome terraces overlooked the valley in the centre of the town. However their stay by the seaside was to no avail as Margaret died on 16 September of *Phthisis Pulmonalis* (pulmonary tuberculosis or consumption) a few months short of her forty-second birthday, leaving Arthur a widower for the second time.

By 1858 the family had moved to Silver Street House, a little way from Taunton town centre on the Corfe road. The house is a fine large eighteenth century house with grey rendering, now used as offices, but towards the end of the century Arthur's youngest son John remembered it as a fine Queen Anne house of red brick which belonged to the adjoining convent. The house itself had its faults, having been neglected, with a badly leaking roof and no drainage. The 1861 Census records that in addition to Arthur as head of the household there were eight children: Downing (aged 14), Margaret (12), Sarah (11), William Arthur (9), Mary (8), George (6), John (4) and Ellen (2). Arthur's 24 year-old niece Anne Davis was present in the role of governess and there were three servants living in – nursemaid Elizabeth Saturley (aged 22, born in Taunton), housemaid Sarah Long (25, born in Dunster on the northern fringes of Exmoor) and cook Martha Reed (26, from West Buckland to the south west of Taunton,). The poor condition of the house probably did not help the children's health. Whether this was a factor is not known but sadly there was yet more tragedy when in 1864 the eldest son Downing died, leaving his father twice-widowed with seven children aged 5 to 15.

Chapter Seven
The Somerset Archaeological & Natural History Society

A S SOON AS HE MOVED TO TAUNTON Jones immersed himself in the civic life of the town at the same time as ministering to his congregation, just as he had done in Northampton and Bridgwater. It was while living in Bridgwater that he joined

7.1: The New Market House, Taunton where SANHS was based before the Castle. (SANHS)

the newly-formed Somerset Archaeological and Natural History Society (henceforth referred to as SANHS or the Society). This had been set up by a group of landed gentry and clergyman in the county in 1849 for 'the cultivation of, and collecting information on, Archaeology and Natural History, in their various branches, but more particularly in connection with the County of Somerset'. A questionnaire was sent to clergymen and others in the county asking them to identify archaeological sites and churches of interest. Although he is not recorded as replying to this questionnaire Jones is included in the first list of members along with twenty nine other Bridgwater residents, including William Baker, the general secretary of the Society's Natural History Department (The Society had two sections, one for each of its main areas of interest, natural history and archaeology). An annual meeting, lasting two to three days, would be held in one of the main towns in Somerset, when papers on topics of interest were presented and visits made to view archaeological sites and historic buildings in the area. In the early days travel would have often been by train, to reach the venue, and by carriage or horseback on the visits: as over one hundred members often attended a meeting the convoy of carriages must have been quite a sight. Each day usually ended with a dinner at the home of a member who of course being of the upper echelons of society had the facilities to provide for such a large party.[74] The inaugural meeting was held on 26 September 1849 in Taunton at which William Buckland, Doctor of Divinity and geologist from Oxford University (and a man of eccentric tastes) was the main speaker. About 350 people attended the meeting and an adjoining room was set up as a temporary museum.[75] As well as these annual events the Society held *conversationi* (seminars) several times a year at which shorter papers were read.

7.2: Portrait of Arthur Jones in academic pose. (Mary Street Chapel)

On moving to Taunton Jones became even more involved in the Society. At the 5th Annual Meeting in Yeovil on 13 September 1853 he was elected general secretary of the Natural History Department, replacing William Baker who had died. (The Natural History Department had only one but for some reason the Archaeology activities of the Society warranted two general secretaries.) Thirteen years later the Revd Francis Warre resigned as one of the Honorary Secretaries and Jones took over, holding the post for the rest of his life.

In addition to his administrative role in SANHS Jones was an active participant in the field trips that formed an essential part of its annual and other meetings. The fact that he was, one can assume, partly responsible for organising trips and for recording what happened on them probably accounts for the frequent and detailed reports in the Society's *Proceedings* of what he said, including occasions on which his colleagues did not entirely agree with his opinions, albeit in a friendly way. For example, on 13 September 1854 the members visited Cothelstone Beacon, one of the high points of the Quantock Hills to the north west of Taunton, where the Revd Francis Warre gave an 'Exposition of the view'.[76]

After describing what could be seen - 'Below us extends the Gwlad-yr-hav, the 'summerfields' of the celtic poets, which with the heights of the Quantocks and the northern coast of Somerset, was the residence of the

7.3: A view from Cothelstone Hill across central Somerset. (Nick Chipchase)

western Cangi'.- he referred to Arthur Jones's view on the meaning of 'Gwlad-yr-Havren':

> I am well aware that my learned friend and colleague, Mr. Jones, will tell you that the "summer-field" is a false translation of the Celtic name, and that Gwlad-yr-havren simply signifies "the land on the coast of the Severn" and it would, indeed, be presumptuous in me to doubt the correctness of his interpretation, but when I look down on that beautiful plain, I hope to be excused (for the day at least), I hold the more poetical translation to be the right one, and believe with Harne, that the Cangi named that beautiful vale and plain "the laughing summer-field".

Jones was a regular and frequent speaker at SANHS meetings. Altogether he gave 12 papers to annual meetings and a further 22 to *conversazioni*. The topics were wide-ranging, roughly equally split between geology and history/archaeology. [see Appendix 3 for a full list as recorded in the SANHS *Proceedings*]. Most were about the Taunton area and West Somerset but he also spoke on more general scientific matters. At a *conversazione* in November 1855 the microscope and some of its uses were his subject, followed in January of the next year with consideration of its application to archaeology and natural history.[77] In November 1856 the French metrical system received his attention. Being particularly interested in this issue he was a corresponding member of the International Association for Obtaining a Uniform System of Measures, Weights and Coins which published his paper as a pamphlet.[78]

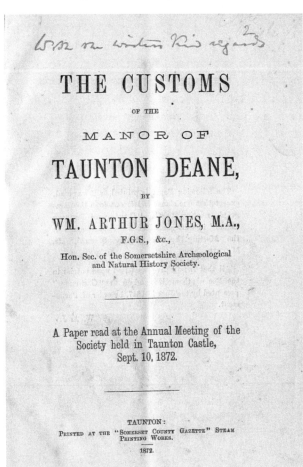

7.4: Customs of Taunton Deane – the cover of a paper by Jones and inscribed by him.. (Dr Adrian Webb)

The *conversazioni* speakers and their topics are recorded in the SANHS *Proceedings* but without the text. Fortunately the local press was sometimes very happy to publish not only the text but also information about who was present and some details of the discussion that took place. This helps the researcher as the original text does not always survive and where it does it might not be readable: William Sanford gave a paper entitled 'On Glaciers' at a *conversazione* on 14 November 1859. The writing in his manuscript copy in the Sanford archives is so poor as to be almost indecipherable but this did not stop the Taunton Courier from publishing the text, albeit a week later than intended![79]

This is not the place to go into detail on all of Jones's many papers, but his first is particularly worthy of note, both for its subject matter and for what it shows of his approach to historical research. It was given to the Society at its meeting in Yeovil in September 1853, held in the Town

Hall which, in the words of the *Somerset County Gazette*, 'was fitted up with great taste for the occasion, and at one end was a well-stored museum, to which the inhabitants of Yeovil and the surrounding neighbourhood largely contributed'.[80] After the usual business matters had been considered papers were presented. Two of them, on Anglo-Saxon and German Romanesque architecture by Mr H.G. Tomkins and on the churches of Normandy by the Revd. W.H. Turner, were on similar themes but Jones's paper was rather different. Drawing on his knowledge of geology and, as a fluent Welsh speaker, of Celtic languages, he aimed to show that the battle of Llongborth, in which the British forces were led by Arthur and in which Geraint, the prince of Dyvnaint or Devon was slain, took place at Langport in the heart of Somerset and not at Portsmouth to which it was normally assigned by scholars. Going back to his source, the *Elegy upon Geraint ab Erbyn* by the Prince-Poet LLywarch Hen, he examined Celtic and Saxon place names and the detailed physical characteristics of the area such as sea-level changes, river and tidal regimes and alluvial deposits. He concluded that 'the battle, celebrated by Llywarch Hen, was fought at Langport in this county, and not at Portsmouth'. Was Jones correct in this conclusion? There is no record of the reaction to his paper from his audience, but it is worth noting that later scholars think that the place-name evidence he uses is unconvincing.[81] The paper is interesting also in that Jones emphasises what he sees as the great potential of non-documentary evidence, often based on field-work, in historical studies:

> It would not be out of place to call attention to the fact that there are very few peculiar and characteristic features in any locality, whether physical or archaeological, which may not, some time or other, become available for the solution and illustration of historical problems, that would otherwise remain obscure.

Judging by reports in the *Somerset County Gazette* (which admittedly could have been written by Jones) his audiences found Jones's papers not only very informative and erudite, but also sometimes witty, illustrated with inventive visual aids or full of the Welshman's poetic imagination, as shown in the following three examples.

At the Annual Meeting in 1859:
A copy of the catalogue of a library which once existed over the chapel at the Vicar's close, at Wells, was forwarded to the meeting by Mr R. Neville Grenville. Some of its items were read by the Rev. W. A. Jones and caused considerable amusement.[82]

From a paper on Cephalopods, or Molluscs of the cuttlefish tribe in 1854:
The very curious apparatus by which the Nautilus Pompilius, and Spiralis Australis are enabled to descend with ease and rapidity to the lowest depths of the sea, and rise again, was fully explained. This power was beautifully illustrated by an hydraulic apparatus which Mr. Jones had prepared, in which fossil ammonite shells were made to float, to descend, and rise again to the surface, according to the same principle which applied to them while living. [83]

From a paper on 'The geology and antiquities of the Mendip Hills' in 1857:
In tracing the history of this district, I must ask you in imagination to accompany me up the vale of Time to a period when no geological formation existed more recent than that of the Devonian rocks.
I shall never forget the visions which passed before my own mind's eye when, after several hours ' patient search, and scrutinising observation on every rock and crevice, and crumbled stone at Cheddar, I threw myself down upon the green sod, amid the silent solitudes of that rocky chasm. The deep shadows from the cliffs above grew deeper and darker, they spread further and wider until all the hills around seemed

enveloped on darkness, and the hills and dells of Somerset were as if they were not. The great powers and agencies of nature seemed to pass before me and by their mysterious working through untold ages proclaimed the might and majesty of His wisdom by whom all things were guided to such glorious and benificent issues. Early that morning I had stood upon the marls of the new red sandstone below the village of Cheddar. I had passed over the earlier magnesian conglomerate limestone which skirts the base of the Mendip-hill. I had seen the lias of the Polden-hills stretch before me, and the Tor of Glastonbury capped with its upper and lower oolite. The green sand of our Blagdon-hills, and the chalk formations above Stourton with almost all the intermediate geological links from the early Devonian rocks of Quantock, had been embraced in the extensive prospect visible from the heights above Cheddar. But now they had all disappeared; even the solid rock of the mountain limestone upon which I rested was gone. The Mendips as yet had no being. The waves of a tropical sea moved restlessly where the solid walls of rock now stood so firm (and much more in the same vein).[84]

Jones's research included a long-term project exploring the Blake family pedigree and he continued to correspond on this subject with the antiquary Sir Thomas Phillips. At times this research was carried out under extreme conditions: during one winter he had to sit in the freezing church at Bishops Hull looking at documents, a far cry from the comfort and facilities of today's county record offices! [85]

His SANHS activities and his research interests brought Jones into contact with local people of like mind, in particular William Ayshford Sanford and Charles Moore. It would seem that Jones had closer ties with Sanford than with Moore despite their very different family backgrounds. The Sanfords had lived at Nynehead Court, a few miles to the south west of Taunton, since about 1590 and owned much of the parish of Nynehead and land elsewhere. The family had provided two MPs and five High Sheriffs of the county. William was born in 1818 and after studying at Cambridge had led an interesting and varied life. He had joined the Camden Society and developed skills as an architect, designing schools in Western Australia, where he was Colonial Secretary in the early 1850s, and the extension to the village church in Nynehead in 1869. He was a palaeontologist and botanist and published a paper on the *Felis* species.[86] He was for a time a secretary of the Society and later its president, as his father Edward Ayshford Sanford had been. Both Sanfords had been founder members although William was probably more scientifically orientated than his father.

The geologist Charles Moore (1814-1881) was a Somerset man born in Ilminster and like Arthur Jones was a Unitarian. He amassed a major collection of fossils, now mainly housed in the Royal Bath Literary and Scientific Institution, and presented a major paper to the Society in 1866 'On the Middle and Upper Lias'. [87] In this he named a fossil after Jones.

"*TURBO JONESEI*'.

Shell turreted, tapering; apex acute; volutions 8, having on their centre two raised nodulated transverse carinae, the lower rather than the largest, and between which is a caniculated area. Above the carina the shell is angulated, and at the base of the whorl is a small encircling nodulated rib. The surface also possesses very fine and close longitudinal striae. From the Upper Lias at Compton. We have but two examples, both of which are partly concealed by the matrix but not quite perfect. It is named after our friend W.A. Jones, F.G.S., of Taunton, one of the Honorary Secretaries of the Somersetshire Archaeological and Natural History Society'.

Turbo jonesei Moore is now considered to be a synonym of *Turbo capitaneus* in the genus *Eucyclus* Deslongchamp but the whereabouts of Moore's original specimen is not known.[88] Moore's paper also shows that by this time Jones's particular interest in geology had already been recognised: he was elected a Fellow of the Geological Society of London in 1858, one of his proposers being Dr James Yates.

7.5: *Turbo jonesei* – engraving of the fossil collected and named by Charles Moore. (SANHS)

There were also foreign contacts. In 1853 there was a visit to Taunton by the Revd Charles Henry Brigham, a congregational minister from the town's namesake in Massachusetts and a leading member of the Old Colony Historical Society. Brigham was on a year-long tour of the principal cities of the 'Old World', making reports on his travels from week to week which were published in the Massachusetts journal known as the *Whig*. His visit to Taunton clearly made a strong impression on him as it was said in his obituary that 'the collection of these letters would make a large volume of records of travel, including interesting historical sketches of ancient Taunton, England . . .'.[89] In one of his letters published in the *Whig* Brigham describes his visits to Blake family properties at Bishops Hull and Holway on the edge of Taunton.[90] He kept in touch with Jones after his return to Massachusetts, and in January 1856 the latter was unanimously chosen to be a corresponding member of the American society. There was an exchange of documents of historical interest but Brigham's letters to Jones also touch on political matters, reflecting another of his interests. In a letter of 21 April 1856 he discusses the state of the anti-slavery movement while on 15 September he comments on the presidential election campaign then under way. He also asks if a letter addressed to the magistrates in Taunton on the subject of international peace had arrived. Other possible visitors to Taunton from Massachusetts were commended to Jones, including Charles G. Crocker ('a young parishioner of mine'), the Revd. R.C. Waterston of Boston, his wife and daughter ('a particular friend of mine and one of those metropolitan ministers who have suffered in popularity from their bold advocacy of the anti-slavery reform'), and Edward Sanford, the son of the Revd Enoch Sanford of Raynham, ('a neighbour and friend of mine'). It is not known if any of these actually arrived in Taunton.[91]

Not surprisingly fieldwork played an important role in Jones's life. William Baker recorded in his paper to SANHS in 1852 on 'The Cannington Park Limestone' that:

> Since I read my paper in Taunton, and the discovery of molluscus shells in this Limestone has been otherwise mentioned, the Rev. W. A. Jones, of Taunton, and Mr. Moore, of Ilminster, in a brief search amongst some heaps of this stone, by the roadside near Bridgwater, cracked out three or four tolerably good specimens of distinct species of bivalve shells.[92]

Jones had taken part in the excavation of a Roman villa at Pitney which had brought to light a beautiful tesselated floor. The site had been discovered in 1828-1829 and had been extensively excavated by Samuel Hasell of Littleton. More recently the excavation had been directed by a Mr Fry of Curry Rivel but at the visit to the site held as part of the Annual Meeting in Langport in August 1861 it was Jones who spoke about the finds (as noted at some length in the *Proceedings*).[93] This was not the only encounter he had with Roman mosaics. A few months later, in October, he had occasion to write to Francis Dickinson, a fellow member of the Society:

> Warre and I propose being at Langport <u>tomorrow</u> by the train that is due there at 11.43 a.m. and intend going on <u>direct</u> to the newly discovered Roman pavement, lying somewhere between Low Ham and High Ham. I hope you will be able to meet us there. I have just given an artist instructions to be there tomorrow by the 1st train, to make an accurate sketch for the Society.[94]

It should be added that this discovery is not to be confused with the Low Ham mosaic in the Museum of Somerset, not discovered until 1938.

The Annual Meeting in Taunton in September 1872 included a visit to see a quarry at Hestercombe, just to the north of Taunton. Until relatively recently Hestercombe House was best known for its early twentieth century garden designed by Edwin Lutyens and Gertrude Jekyll, but to the north of the house, in a combe leading up into the lower slopes of the Quantocks, lies an eighteenth century landscape garden which has in the last few years been restored and opened to the public. A path up the left side of the combe, past lakes and an artificial waterfall, leads to a small quarry where igneous formations, described on the visit by Jones and Boyd Dawkins, the eminent geologist

7.6: Rock exposure in the quarry in the eighteenth century garden at Hestercombe, Taunton. (AC)

and honorary member of the Society, can be seen, at least in winter when they are not concealed by vegetation.

Jones also took the opportunity when out on family business to investigate the local geology and wildlife.[95] It has already been mentioned that in May 1860 Jones took his sick wife Margaret to Dawlish on the south Devon coast where it was hoped she would benefit from the sea air. Here, in addition to caring for her he found time to explore the fauna and flora of the seashore and to send specimens to William Sanford.[96i]

In 1862 he was involved in what we would now call 'rescue archaeology'. Until the early nineteenth century excavations had been confined largely to barrows and similar features not particularly under threat. The coming of the railways changed this. The earthworks that were required to build the lines endangered known sites and revealed new ones, and the need to take action either to preserve remains or more often to remove artefacts of interest was soon recognised. During the construction of the Taunton to Watchet Railway Jones retrieved a large collection of Romano-British pottery found near Norton Fitzwarren, just to the west of Taunton, which he presented to the Society's museum. The discoveries were made during the construction of the bridge which now takes the B3227 road from Taunton over the railway and west towards Wiveliscombe. The site of the discovery was marked on the 1st edition of the 25 inches to the mile Ordnance Survey map where it is shown as a fishpond: it is indeed still used for fishing. The need for swift action was brought to Jones's attention by Charles Welman of nearby Norton Manor, across whose land the railway was to run. Having met the foreman who showed him the site Jones organised the excavations, taking along a group of young archaeologists.[97] The pottery found is now in the Museum of Somerset collection. In his report to the Annual Meeting in Wellington on 20 August the secretary Francis Warre said there was a lesson to be learnt from this:

> The fact that this extensive series of specimens, so valuable for illustration, would in all probability have been buried under the railway if the collection of them had been sufficiently delayed only twenty-four hours, affords a sufficient ground to your Committee for urging members of the Society to make prompt and careful observations wherever works of this character are being executed.[98]

The Society's Museum

In the early days of the Society a museum had been established on a temporary basis at the New Market House on the west side of the Parade in Taunton. Items of interest were also displayed at the Annual Meetings, with the Society's *Proceedings* recording the items donated and displayed. Jones was involved in the early days of the museum and played a major role in some of its major acquisitions. One of the most important of these was the collection of fossils from the caves at Banwell, where the M5 now crosses the Mendips, and which overlook Weston-super-Mare and the Bristol Channel. The Stalactite and Bone caves at Banwell had been discovered in 1757 and 1824 respectively, the latter being especially attractive to a public which included many distinguished geologists and clerics, including William Buckland, Richard Owen, Roderick Murchison and the Revd John Keble.[99] Jones shared an interest in the caves with William Sanford and gave a paper on the bone caves to the Society in 1857.[100] He visited the caves in September of that year, for which he paid an entry fee of 1s, and again in November 1860, this time accompanied by Sanford and Edward Parfitt (of the 'Taunton Society' according to the visitors book).[101] The collection of bones had been put together by

William Beard who, in August 1862 and now an old man of over 90 years, wrote to Jones (presumably) that 'I believe my splendid collection will be sold soon after my death, unless I sell it before'.[102] Jones put forward a scheme whereby the Society would invite subscriptions for the purchase and by the Annual Meeting in Burnham in 1864 the bones had been successfully acquired.

Items donated to the museum came not only from Somerset but also from much further afield. On 8 July 1871 Charles Brooke, the second Rajah of Sarawak, wrote advising that he had dispatched various items for the museum by the Barque *Alcestis*. In a barrel were 'flying lemurs, white marked squirrels, small deer, a white kind of rat, a small alligator, a young maias [the Malay for an orang-utan] and one or two others the names of which I do not know'.[103] Entrusted to the captain was a shield. Some of these and more are recorded as donations to the museum: 'Alligator's skull and claws, skin of boa, tortoise shell, Dyak war jackets, women's petticoats, waist cloths, seat mat, earrings, armlets, war charms, spear heads, spikes, swords, and shield, from H.H. THE RAJAH OF SARAWAK'. Brooke had Somerset connections. He was the son of the Revd Charles Johnson, vicar of White Lackington near Ilminster, and his wife Emma (née Brooke) and it is possible he made contact with Jones and the Society in 1869 when he returned to England to marry Margaret de Windt of Wiltshire. He was certainly interested in museums, having founded the Sarawak Museum, which was mainly for zoological specimens, but which also embraced anthropology and folk art.

7.7: A sestertius of Antoninus Pius (Emperor AD 138-61); found on the Mendips and given to the museum by Jones. (Museum of Somerset)

Jones contributed many items himself to the SANHS museum (See Appendix 4). He pursued his interest in the natural world and mankind's past by collecting geological specimens and artefacts. The present-day Museum of Somerset records contain 16 items of fossils and rocks that he obtained both locally and further afield, including igneous rock from Hestercombe near Taunton, a *Gorgonia verrucosa* from Seaton in east Devon and Silurian fossils from Llandeilo in Carmarthenshire. He also donated many items not geological in nature – the museum today lists 25 - including an ancient teapot with the legend 'no cider tax, apples at liberty'; a milking stool, dug from an old filled up water course under old houses in St. James's Street in Taunton, and, intriguingly, 'The Battle of Sedgemoor, Rehearst at White hall, a farce'. The last of these had been exhibited but presumably not performed at the local museum in Langport during the 13th Annual Meeting in 1861.

The previous thirty years had seen much interest in dinosaurs both locally and nationally. In 1859 in his report about the museum William Sanford, then President of the Society said that:

> The only fossil of importance we have received during this year is a portion of the skeleton of a very large ichthyosaurus, from Stoke St Mary, the first I believe found in that locality. For this we are indebted to the kindness of Mr. Arthur Jones, our excellent secretary.[104]

This was one of Jones's most important contributions to the museum. The fossil is still in the Museum of Somerset's collection, but it is not clear whether Jones himself excavated it.

The Society's museum was not only the recipient of noteworthy specimens: it was also a source of information for other researchers. The palaeontologist Hugh Falconer (1808-1865) was especially interested in the contents of what he called 'ossiferous caves', such as Kent's Hole at Torquay, caves at Brixham and on the Gower in south Wales, and at Banwell. His *Palaeontological Memoirs and Notes*, edited by Charles Murcheson, include a 'note on the occurrence of spermophilus in the cave fauna of England'. Falconer recorded that:

> In 1859, while examining the rich collection of fossil bones, made by the late Dr Daniel [sic] Williams, from the numerous caves of the Mendip hills, and now preserved in the Museum of the Somersetshire Literary and Philosophical Society at Taunton, I detected two rami of the lower jaw of a species of Spermophilus, which by the kindness of the Rev. W. Arthur Jones, I was enabled to compare with recent specimens in the metropolitan collections.[105]

The Society was faced with donations to its museum of a great variety of items, some of which would be relatively unknown, so it is not surprising that their acquisition did not always go smoothly. In 1865 a Mr Wookey gave the museum 'a young gorilla from Africa'. On 4 November of that year Jones wrote to William Sanford for help with a particularly sensitive matter:

> The company of the Gorilla is becoming very unpleasant – to use the mildest term, and it will be necessary to decide on Monday next what we are to do with him. I have arranged with Tuckwell to have the case opened in the College School garden at 12 o'clock next Monday. I hope you will be able to come in and give us the benefit of your judgement in the matter.[106]

Mr Tuckwell was the headmaster of the Taunton College School. At this time the school occupied what are now the municipal buildings on Corporation Street in Taunton and looked across Castle Green to the museum.

Chapter Eight
Two Years in the Pyrenees

ARTHUR JONES'S LIFE IN TAUNTON came to an abrupt end in October 1866 when he surprised his Mary Street congregation by announcing that he was leaving Taunton for the south of France. A letter of 2 October to his congregation explained his decision:

> You will be sorry to hear that I am obliged to leave Taunton on account of the health of members of my family, to spend the winter in the South of France. I am advised and urged to do this without delay by Medical Practitioners of the highest eminence. I am anxious that you should all know this as early as possible – from myself directly, and not from strangers. I most deeply regret to have to leave you on so short a notice, but having now for very many years had so many proofs of your kindness I do not for a moment doubt but that you will cheerfully put up with any inconvenience that may arise from my being obliged to leave you so hastily and so unexpectedly. Our Congregational Committee, (in conjunction with myself before I leave, and with several Ministerial Friends in the district after) will, I have no doubt, be able to provide until my return, for the Ministrations which, I am obliged unhappily for a time to give up.[107]

He set out his reasons in more detail in a letter two days later to William Blake.[108] It was the health of his daughter Margaret which was giving most cause for concern, but two or three others in the family were also affected. Pleurisy was mentioned but the move to France was for prevention rather than cure. He felt that the outlay would be a

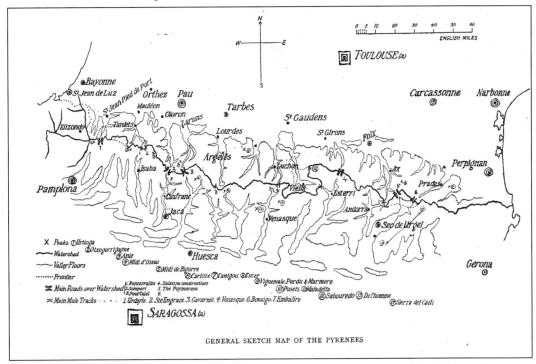

GENERAL SKETCH MAP OF THE PYRENEES

8.1: General Sketch Map of the Pyrenees. One of two maps from 'The Pyrenees' by Hilaire Belloc. (Reprinted by permission of Peters Fraser & Dunlop on behalf of the Estate of Hilaire Belloc)

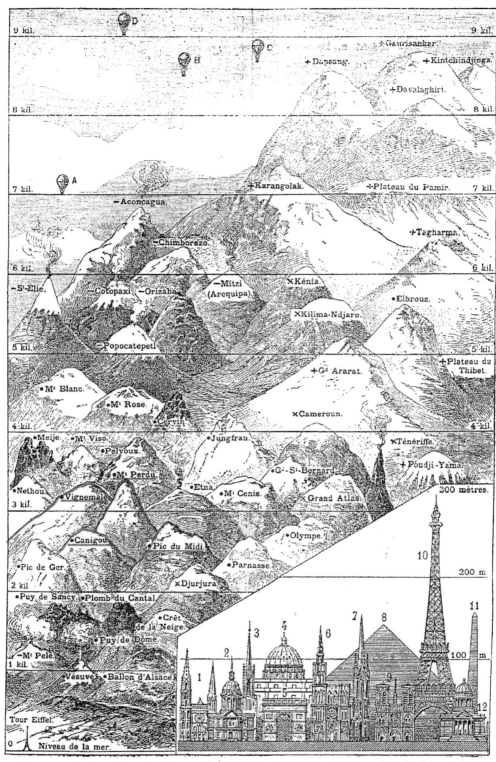

MONTAGNES. — Le signe . indique les montagnes d'Europe; le signe + celles d'Asie; le signe — celles de l'Amérique; le signe ✕ celles de l'Afrique. — ASCENSIONS CÉLÈBRES : A, Gay-Lussac (1804); B, Sivel et Crocé-Spinelli (1874); C, Tissandier, Sivel et Crocé-Spinelli (1875); D, Berson (1894). — MONUMENTS : 1. Cathédrale de Chartres; 2. Les Invalides (Paris); 3. Cathédrale de Rouen; 4. Saint-Pierre de Rome; 5. L'Arc de triomphe de l'Etoile; 6. La cathédrale de Strasbourg; 7. La cathédrale de Cologne; 8. La grande pyramide d'Egypte; 9. Notre-Dame de Paris; 10. La tour Eiffel; 11. L'obélisque de Washington; 12. Le Panthéon (Paris).

8.2: The Pyrenees compared with other mountain ranges. The Pyrenean peaks are outlined in red. (*Le Petit Larousse Illustré*, 1908)

good investment and that the visit would do them much good educationally although his doctor (Dr Symonds) 'has forbidden close application to study'. It was also suggested much later that a disagreement with a Mr Preston about a church outing might have been a factor in the move.[109] Initially the Mary Street congregation was expecting him to return after perhaps one winter in France, but he formally resigned his post in February 1867 and the chapel had to find a new minister.

The local press reported the announcement, suggesting that it was not completely out of the blue as it was known that the Jones children, or at least some of them, were not in the best of health. The *Dictionary of National Biography*, both the original entry and the recent revision, covers this stage of Jones's life in a single sentence (he was 'travelling for two years on the continent') but these few words conceal a period of intense activity which went far beyond looking after the well-being of his large family. Only eight days after telling his congregation that he was leaving Jones wrote to William Sanford that 'we have finally settled to leave for the South of France this day week the 17th inst'. The family's destination was the Pyrenees mountain range on the border between France and Spain, and in particular the town of Pau in the (then) Basse-Pyrénées department of France. His initial intention was 'to go to Pau or Bigorres [Bagnères-de Bigorre] and then determine by experience'. He was not taking any servants but Miss Hollins (the children's governess) was to accompany them: 'The children are all delighted, and Sarah [his second daughter] more than satisfied'.[110]

Why did Arthur Jones choose the Pyrenees?

It was not unusual for Britons to seek the sun in the south of France or in Italy, and the Pyrenees in particular would have held many attractions for someone of Arthur Jones's wide-ranging interests. In the late eighteenth century interest in romantic and sublime landscapes focussed on the mountains, which came to be seen as places worthy of visit, not places to be avoided as they had been. There was also a growth of interest in the sci-

Les Pyrénées Illustrées.

593. — Pau. - Le Château et le Boulevard du Midi vus de la Saligue.

8.3: Pau from the Gave, showing the château on the left of the picture. (AC)

entific aspects of mountains, in their geology and in their wildlife. In comparison with the Alps, which also attracted much interest, the Pyrenees might not be considered to be a major mountain range: the Alps rise to 15,771 ft whilst the crest of the Pyrenees is marked by a series of peaks of a little over 10,000ft. There has been a long running rivalry between the two areas which continues today, a rivalry epitomised by contrasting quotes from two visitors. On 9 August 1785 the Comte de Guibert (1743-1790) commented, after visiting the Pyrenees:

> *Un voyage des Pyrénées suffit pour donner a une femme une idée des pays des montagnes; mais un homme qui veut connaitre, un homme qui doit préférer les grandes masses aux détails, et les superbes horreurs aux charmes d'un paysage, un homme que les fatigues et les difficultés ne doivent pas rebuter, doit préférer d'aller contempler et étudier la nature dans les Alpes.*[111]

In other words, the Pyrenees are fine for introducing women to mountains, but real men go to the Alps! In contrast, a century later Henri Brulle (1854-1936) was scathing about what he saw as the limited appeal of the Alps in contrast to what the Pyrenees offered:

> *L'alpinisme, c'est l'escalade. Pyrénéeisme, c'est moins l'esprit sportif que l'anime que la soif de la solitude et de la liberté, l'attrait du pittoresque, de l'aventure, la pénétration dans la mystère des aspects sacrés de la nature.*[112]

That is, the Pyrenees are about things of the spirit and the mysteries of the natural world: the Alps are just about climbing mountains!

Interest in the Pyrenees as a place for scientific study was stimulated at the turn of the nineteenth century by the French scientist Louis-François Elisabeth Ramond de Carbonnières, who explored the mountains and recorded their wildlife. The British too became frequent visitors and major explorers of the region. There had been British visitors to the Pyrenees since at least 1740 but in the nineteenth century they were increasingly attracted by the opportunities for sightseeing, scientific and historical study, health (the area is noted for its spas), painting and sketching and mountain climbing. The first recorded ascent by a tourist of le Vignemale, at 1,0824ft the highest peak in the French Pyrenees, was in fact by a Yorkshire woman, Ann Lister, accompanied by guides, in 1838.[113]

Pau

The town of Pau lies just to the north of the Pyrenean foothills, about 60 miles from the sea at Biarritz. Historically it was very important being at various times the capital of the ancient provinces of Béarn and of Navarre, whose parliament building can still be seen in the town. Today it is the chief town of the Pyrénées-Atlantique Département, a lively commercial centre and home to a university. The historic core of the town is the sixteenth century château and birthplace of Henri IV of France which stands beside a network of narrow streets and sits on a bluff overlooking, to the south, the Gave de Pau ['Gave' is the local name for a river], which rises high in the mountains at the renowned Cirque de Gavarnie, near the border with Spain.

British people had been visiting Pau since the mid-eighteenth century but real interest started at the end of the Napoleonic wars. After the battle of Orthez in 1814, when Wellington defeated Marshal Sault, several of his officers were so attracted to the area that they stayed on. This was the beginning of such an intense immigration that Pau became known as '*la ville anglaise*'. It has been estimated that in the early 1860s about 15%

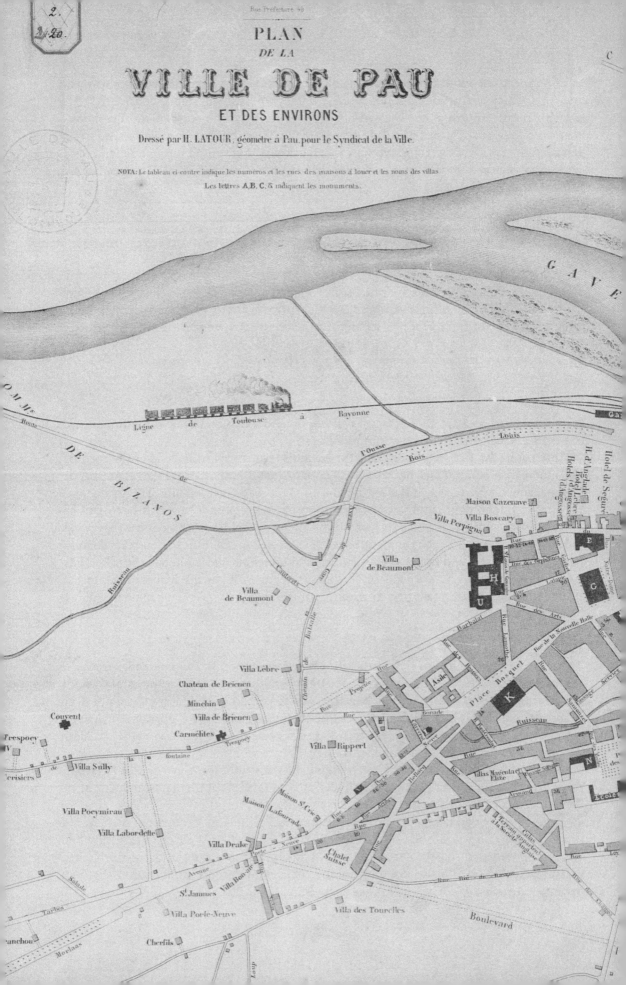

PLAN
DE LA
VILLE DE PAU
ET DES ENVIRONS

Dressé par H. LATOUR, géomètre à Pau, pour le Syndicat de la Ville.

NOTA: Le tableau ci-contre indique les numéros et les rues des maisons à louer et les noms des villas

Les lettres **A**, **B**, **C**, & indiquent les monuments.

GAVE

Ligne de Toulouse à Bayonne

Route de BIZANOS

Maison Cazenave

Villa Boscary

Villa Perpigna

Villa de Beaumont

Villa de Beaumont

Villa Lèbre

Chateau de Bricnen

Minchin

Villa de Bricnen

Couvent

Carmélites

Trespoey

Villa Sully

Villa Rippert

Maison St Cric

Maison Lafourcade

Villa Poeymirau

Villa Labordette

Villa Drake

Chalet Suisse

St Jammes

Villa Bonan

Villa Porte-Neuve

Villa des Tourelles

Boulevard

Hotel de Ségur

Place Bosquet

Asile

Ecole

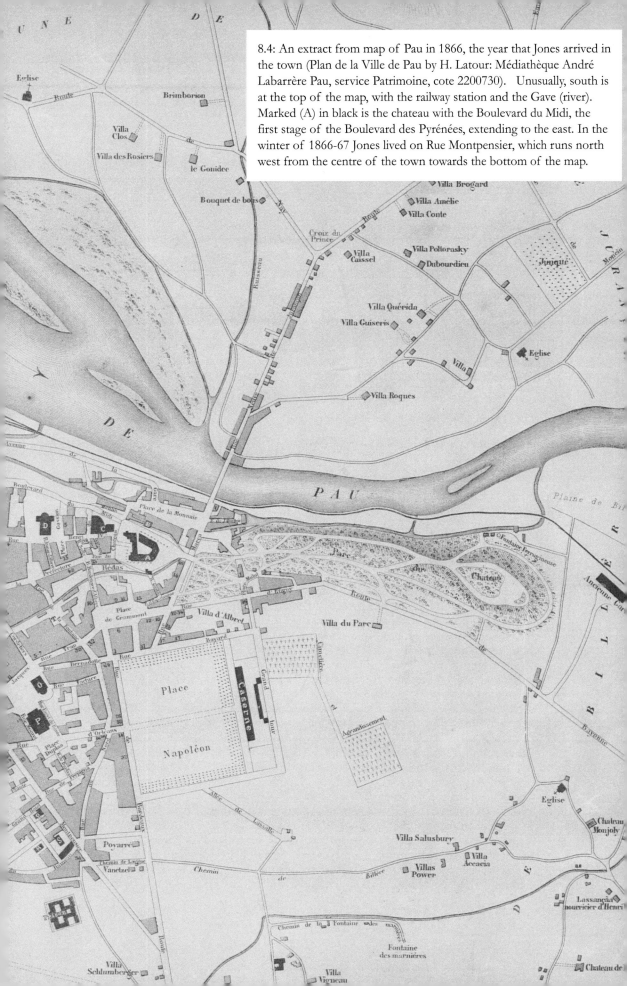

8.4: An extract from map of Pau in 1866, the year that Jones arrived in the town (Plan de la Ville de Pau by H. Latour: Médiathèque André Labarrère Pau, service Patrimoine, cote 2200730). Unusually, south is at the top of the map, with the railway station and the Gave (river). Marked (A) in black is the chateau with the Boulevard du Midi, the first stage of the Boulevard des Pyrénées, extending to the east. In the winter of 1866-67 Jones lived on Rue Montpensier, which runs north west from the centre of the town towards the bottom of the map.

8.5: The Pyrenees from Pau, from an old postcard. (AC)

of the population was English.[114] The attraction of the Pau area was eloquently described in 1843 by Georges-Williams Lefèvre (in *The life of a travelling Physician from his first introduction to practice; including 20 years wanderings through the greater part of Europe*). Lefèvre was born in England and trained as a doctor in Scotland, but his family were probably Huguenots from the south west of France. He was accompanying Lord Selkirk's party on a journey through the south of France, arriving in Pau on 30 September 1819:

> As the day after our arrival proved to be fine, we took a ride to reconnoitre, and seldom have my eyes been more astonished at the majesty of nature than upon this occasion. Every thing which I had hitherto beheld appeared insignificant compared with the scenery which now presented itself. Immediately before us, and under our feet (for the town is built on abrupt ridges), extended a long plain of meadow land, through which the Gave serpentined in a quick and bubbling stream. The fore ground was bounded by a long ridge of hills covered with the vines festooning from their summits to their feet; and these were backed again by forest trees, among which the beech predominated; and to bound the whole, the Pyrenees stretching along the horizon, resembled, by their rugged summits, the back bone of the globe. The four seasons seemed to be blended into each other, and present at the same time. The meadows still wore the aspect of spring. The hills covered with the rich luxuriant grape, in its mature state, indicated the influence of the summer's sun; the blood-red beech and other forest trees began to show, in their party-coloured leaves, the garments of autumn; and, lastly, the snow-capped mountains presented all the dreariness of winter, save when for a few moments they were illumined by the rays of a setting sun, which had already left the plains in darkness.
> From the centre of the long ridge, rose in perpendicular form, higher and more conical in shape than the rest, the Pic du Midi. From the distance at which we then viewed it, it appeared as if insulated from the rest of the chain, and its conical and slender-looking pic was frequently hidden by some hovering cloud, when the less towering heads of its neighbours were distinctly visible. The sight of all this grandeur determined the party upon making Pau their winter quarters.

Even today visitors to Pau will recognise this description. The view of the Pyrenees chain from the Boulevard des Pyrénées, which extends along the southern side of the town overlooking the Gave, is one of the town's major attractions for tourists, although at the time of Jones's visit only the western part of the Boulevard had been built: it was extended to the east after 1872.

The second boost to foreign interest in Pau came towards the middle of the nineteenth century. This part of France had long been noted for its relaxing atmosphere but in 1842 a Scottish doctor and Pau resident, Alexander Taylor, published a study with the cumbersome title of *Climates for invalides: or, a comparative enquiry as to the preventative and curative influences of the climate of Pau, and of Montpellier, Hyères, Nice, Rome, Pisa, Florence, Naples, Biarritz, etc. on health and disease.* In this he concluded that, on the basis of comparative death rates, Pau was the healthiest place of those likely to be visited by the British and other foreigners.[116] Although his conclusions were to be challenged a few years later the book had a major effect on the number of people coming to stay in Pau primarily for the winter (known in French as *'les hivernais'*); it was common practice among the British and other visitors to move up to the hills and mountains to avoid the summer heat.

The local newspaper, *Le Mémorial des Pyrénées*, regularly published lists of foreign visitors arriving in the town. Usually it concentrated on the aristocracy but on 2 January 1848 it published a census of foreign residents (*étrangers*), which showed the dominance of the British. Of the total of 644 foreigners recorded 334 were described as *'anglais'*, of whom 199 were *'maîtres'* and 135 *'domestiques'*.[117] This expatriate British community developed a strong social life, with a club, churches, sporting activities, hunting and even a book society.

In 1863 a railway to Pau was built from Dax on the Paris to Biarritz line. This made a great difference to the accessibility of the town for the British, bringing the Pyrenees within 36 hours of London. Before the advent of railways the mountains were reached either by a long land journey via Paris or by ship to Bordeaux, followed by an uncomfortable passage across the Landes by diligence, if one didn't have access to a private carriage.[118] Pau in the last forty years of the nineteenth century therefore became a focus for British visitors, with the building of many hotels and villas and completion of the Boulevard des Pyrénées. Several people from Somerset or with Somerset connections were among those who made their way to the area, especially during the latter half of the nineteenth century and in the early twentieth century. Among them were William Sanford of Nynehead Court, who was in Bagnères-de-Bigorre in 1843 on his way to the south of Spain;[119] Elizabeth Clarke of Ashcott near Street, whose monument in the parish church records that she died in Pau on 27 November 1855 aged 77; John Jeffrey Guy Evered J.P. of Otterhampton who ended his days in Pau in 1889; William Gibbs of Tyntesfield, who was in Pau in 1853;[120] Edward A. Freeman of Wells, also active in the Society, who

8.6: The Clarke monument in the church at Ashcott, near Street, Somerset. (AC)

wrote to Jones in 1867 about his experiences in the area;[121] Charlotte Eliza Acland Troyte, who published in 1887 an account of her journey from 'the Pyrenees to Calais in a dog cart'; and the Revd R. Acland-Troyte, in 1914 the chaplain at St Andrew's Anglican church in the rue O'Quin in Pau.[122]

Jones probably learnt of the attractions of the Pyrenees directly from friends and acquaintances. William Sanford's visit in 1843 has already been mentioned. In January 1866 Edward Lewis Knight and his wife Henrietta, sister of William Sanford, wrote to him from the town of Foix in the eastern Pyrenees: he could well have told Jones about this. It was, however, two papers given to SANHS that probably encouraged Jones to go to this part of France.

8.7: Farnham Maxwell Lyte. (Wikipedia)

In March 1856, Farnham Maxwell Lyte (1827-1906) presented a paper to a SANHS *conversazione* entitled 'On photography'. Lyte was the son of the Revd Henry Francis Lyte (best known as the author of the hymn 'Abide with me', who had been the vicar of Brixham in Devon). In February 1851, at Norton Fitzwarren Church just to the west of Taunton, Farnham married Eleanora Julia Bolton. Two years later they moved to the south of France for health reasons, staying there until 1880. Lyte had wide-ranging scientific interests. He was an Associate of the Society of Civil Engineers and a Fellow of the Chemical Society. In the Pyrenees he made meteorological observations, bought a salt-mine and developed armaments at the time of the Franco-Prussian War from 1870 to 1871. However, he was best known for his pioneering work in photography and especially for his landscapes of the Pyrenees, becoming known as '*le père de la photographie pyrénéenne*' (the father of Pyrenean photography). Lyte's photographs were widely exhibited in Europe and, although his paper to SANHS was largely about photographic techniques, it was accompanied by a display of several views of the Pyrenees.[123]

How Lyte came to give this paper is not known. However, his marriage certificate records that Eleanora Bolton was living at the time of their wedding at Norton Manor, home of Charles Welman, a founder member and vice-president of SANHS. Daughter of Cornelius Bolton of County Waterford in Ireland she was in fact born at Trull on the edge of Taunton in 1828 and was possibly a niece of Welman's wife Ann Eliza Bolton. Welman visited the Pyrenees at least twice, in 1860 and 1861, and in January 1862 gave a paper about the Pyrenees to a *conversazione* in which he showed photographs of the area, probably taken by Lyte.[124] Jones would have been present on both occasions so it is not surprising that he found his way to this part of

8.8: Trees in the park at Pau by F.M. Lyte, 1853 (Royal Collection Trust/© Her Majesty Queen Elizabeth II, 2013)

the south of France, rather than one of the other areas favoured by the British such as Nice or Biarritz.

Jones left Taunton with his family and their governess Miss Hollins on 17 October 1866, aiming to arrive in Pau by the 21st. They travelled by train to Southampton where they took the London and South Western Railway's steam packet service, the *S.S. Southampton*, to Le Havre. According to his youngest son John the overnight crossing was:

> Twelve hours and rather rough. Miss Hollins had for the last three weeks been dosing us with things to prevent sea-sickness. We were put in stuffy bunks with rough blankets and no sheets and for first and last time I was very sick throwing it all out of bunk to a red velvet couch below . . .

The family transferred by train to Paris where they stayed at the Hôtel de Lille et d'Albion for two nights before taking the train to Pau, stopping off at Tours and Bordeaux. On arriving in Pau they followed the practice of many visitors in that they stayed at first in a hotel. John Jones recorded that it was in the middle of the town, 'very hot and stuffy', possibly the Hôtel de Commerce with its central courtyard. They then moved to apartments at 39 rue Montpensier on the north side of the town in an area favoured by the Eng-

8.9: The Buddicombe locomotive which was in use on French railways in 1854 (French Embassy)

lish. By the following February they were well settled, as Jones told William Sanford: 'We have a delightful suite of apartments with noble views of the Pyrenees and have 2 trustworthy French servants and more than the usual amounts of comforts around us. For the house I have had to pay a very high rent, but as to provisions etc we find them cheaper than at Taunton and the <u>beef</u> equally good!'.[125] This favourable opinion of the house was at odds with that of his daughter, Margaret, and niece, Edith, who were not impressed with it, at least when compared with where they stayed later.[126]

Jones aimed to immerse his children in the local culture, with the boys going to the local Lycée and two of the girls to a French school. He was pleased that the stay was already having a beneficial effect on the health of his children and he wished to spend time with them rather than with the expatriate community, of which he took a dim view:

> The English visitors at Pau are almost without exception pleasure-seekers with no love for or interest in scientific pursuits so I have had very little communion of that kind and I have preferred the society of my own children to the attractions of the English Club.
> The <u>English</u> inhabitants are so hard up for 'sport' that they have got up a 'paper hunt' on horseback!! They were tired of the 'bag-foxes'! There are not more than three or four besides myself who seem to take any pleasure whatever in scientific pursuits and they seem amazed that my children are made to go on with their education while here! We have made some pleasant acquaintances notwithstanding and as you know we are a large party, with plenty to amuse and occupy ourselves and each other.[127]

THE TARBES VALLEYS & LUCHON

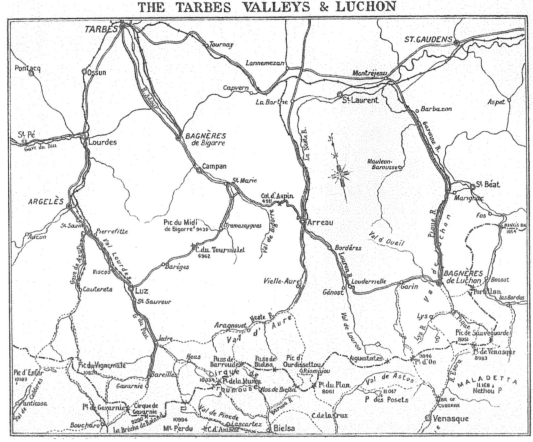

8.10: The Tarbes Valleys and Luchon. One of two maps from 'The Pyrenees' by Hilaire Belloc.
(Reproduced by permission of Peters Fraser & Dunlop on behalf of the Estate of Hilaire Belloc)

As a result, when not at school, the Jones family spent their time exploring the local countryside, painting and studying wildlife:

> We are beginning to fall in with rare plants such as the <u>aphroglossum</u> lusitanicum. Today Sarah is engaged in drawing an exquisite lily – new to us – I find it is the erythronium <u>dens canis</u>. The woods abound with it. Was it not the Desman – the musk rat – you spoke of to me? It is found on the banks of the <u>Adour</u>. Mr. Lyte has promised to get me a specimen if he can. I do not hear that it is found on the <u>Gave</u>.[128]

The family's explorations also included riding in the hills in the wine-growing area of Jurançon, just to the south of Pau, and a trip up the Vallée d'Ossau where they experienced the mountains' winter weather.

In March 1867, accompanied by the governess Miss Hollins, Jones went back to England to deal with family business in Wales and in Norfolk. After a month, on 9 April, he left England to return to Pau, this time with his 21-year old niece Edith, the eldest child of William and Fanny Blake. She stayed with the Jones family until the summer, her detailed weekly letters to her mother providing a valuable additional source of information about their life at this time, as well as insights into her Uncle Arthur's character.[129]

Edith travelled widely in Europe and her letters show her to be 'an educated woman with cultured tastes'.[130] The cross-channel journey was again rough but as before Jones did not seem to be affected. They stayed at the Hôtel Bedford in Paris for several days, visiting the Great Paris Exhibition of 1867. Edith was impressed with the exhibits, remarking particularly on the English farming apparatus on show. She and Jones had different ideas about how to go round and she appears to have been rather fed up with her 49-year old uncle. Although always attentive to the needs of his children he could be somewhat impatient, as she told her mother:

> I am very glad I shall have a chance of seeing it again but Uncle Jones says "Oh! He has seen <u>everything</u> now, and would not at all care to see it again!" It is perfectly ridiculous! Of course we <u>ran</u> through a great deal and know what sort of things are in the parts we passed through, but I don't suppose we saw <u>half</u>, and I don't believe anyone could in 2 days. And then we did not do it in a methodical way, but just walked about anywhere. <u>He</u> always wanted to turn to the <u>left</u> and the consequence was we were always coming round to the same point; however yesterday I made a little plan marking out what he cared most to see (as I should have another chance) and then keeping as nearly as I could to those departments and by that means we got on more satisfactorily.

From Paris they travelled via Poitiers and Bordeaux, arriving in Pau on the morning of Sunday 13 April after a hot and dusty journey. Here life continued much as before, including visits from 'Uncle and Aunt Robberds' (the Revd John and Elizabeth Robberds, William Blake's sister and brother-in-law). Members of the family made two long trips. At the beginning of May, Jones, Edith and his daughters Margaret and Ellen went west to the seaside town of Biarritz in the Basque country where they stayed for a week. Biarritz had been gaining in importance as a resort, largely through the influence of the Empress Eugenie, wife of Napoleon III, who had a villa built there in 1854. The Jones party stayed in more modest lodgings, which did, however, have a sea view. The girls spent their time exploring the local area, and in Edith's case, looking at the local flora with another English visitor, Mr Holland, while Jones took an 11 hour journey by train through the Basque country to the old Castillian capital of Burgos in northern Spain. He was impressed with the landscape and the architecture:

> I made an excursion in Spain as far as Burgos —including Tolosa, Alsasua, Vitoria, Miranda del Ebro, and the pass of Paucorbo. I hardly know which was the more interesting, the journey over the Spanish Pyrenees – including the magnificent scenery about Miranda and the Pass of Pancorbo, or the rich profusion of fine specimens of gothic architecture in and about Burgos.[131]

He made notes about the cathedral of Santa Maria in Burgos, which was the first Gothic cathedral in Spain, building having started in 1221 although most of the work was done in the 15th and 16th centuries.[132] He was not unhappy with the hotel accommodation but the local cuisine was a different matter. It was, he told Edith, bad! We do not know precisely where Jones stayed or which aspects of Spanish cuisine he found particularly distasteful, but it is clear that in his short stay he had in his view an unfortunate experience. This contrasts with that of the English architect George Edmund Street who was travelling in the area in the 1860s. In his account of the journey from Bayonne through Burgos (where he made detailed plans of the cathedral) Street comments that 'So far as the inns and food are to be considered, I do not think there is much need ordinarily for violent grumbling. All ideas of English manners and customs must be carefully left behind; and if the travelling-clothes are donned with a full intention to do in Spain as Spain does, there is small fear of their owner suffering much'. Not all was good however: 'The great objection to these small inns is, that nothing but the linen for the beds and the face of the waiting-maid ever seems to be washed'.[133]

On Jones's return to Biarritz the party went back into Spain, to San Sebastian, and on the way to Pau stopped briefly in the historic town of Bayonne. Then at the beginning of June, Jones, Edith, Sarah and Mary, together with Mr Darke, an English relative of the Robberds, headed south from Pau 30 miles up the Vallée d'Ossau into the heart of the Pyrenees. They had no difficulty in finding rooms at the hotel at Eaux-Chaudes and from there they were able to go even higher up the valley to the foot of the Pic du Midi d'Ossau. One of at least three 'Pics du Midi' in the Pyrenees, this mountain has a very distinctive shape and when the weather is fine (which is by no means always the case) can be clearly seen from Pau. Excursions in the immediate neighbourhood of Pau included a visit to the ancient town of Lescar, about three miles to the west. The town had its origins in Roman times (as Beneharnum) although it was devastated by the Vikings in 841 AD. The core of the town stands on a ridge looking south to the mountains, with at its heart the twelfth century church of Notre Dame, noted for its mosaics.

Argelès-de-Bigorre

On 16 June 1867 the Jones party left Pau and, in common with many other '*hivernais*', headed into the mountains to avoid the summer heat on the plains. Their destination was the town of Argelès-de-Bigorre (now Argelès-Gazost), 30 miles higher up the valley of the Gave de Pau. Bigorre is the ancient name of this part of the Pyrenees, bounded by the provinces of Béarn to the west and Les Comminges to the east. Before the river reaches Lourdes on its way north the valley widens out to form a wide floodplain in which Argelès is the main settlement. Today the late nineteenth and twentieth century parts of the town spread out into the flat areas of the valley but in 1867 the old town was restricted to a site higher up on the western side under the shelter of the 3,600ft high Mont de Gez and had not yet attracted the interest of the British to any significant degree.[134] It was recorded in 1866 as having only 1698 inhabitants but was to grow significantly towards the end of the century.[135]

Jones and his family travelled from Pau by 'omnibus' (probably a diligence) along the Gave, stopping on the way at Lestelle-Betharram where they saw the pilgrims' church

8.11: A diligence – one of the main means of travel for ordinary people in nineteenth century Europe. (*Le Petit Larousse Illustré*, 1908)

and the Stations of the Cross which are marked by a series of chapels up the hill overlooking the village. They would have then passed through Lourdes. It was nine years since Bernadette Soubirous had received her visions of the Virgin Mary at the mouth of the Grotte de Massabielle and the town was already developing as a centre of pilgrimage. Although the first church to provide for the needs of pilgrims was not consecrated until 1874, a statue of the 'Madonna of Lourdes' had been set up in 1864. Surprisingly, therefore, neither Arthur's nor Edith's letters refer to what was happening there. This cannot have been because they were avoiding the town for religious reasons: Edith recorded that they were happy to make the acquaintance of a young priest at the church at St Savin near Argelès.

For their stay in the mountains Jones had found a suitable house, Chalet Lassalle, in Vieuzac, a village adjoining the north side of Argelès. The house was owned by a widow, Mme Lassalle, described thus by Edith:

> Madame Lassalle is a queer old lady! She is Scottish but her husband was French. She has lived here about 20 years and told us she loved this house like her child and was always trying to improve it! So I suppose <u>that</u> is the reason of all the crooks and seats (snuffers and extinguishers too in each room!). Other small conveniences one does not expect to find in a lodging house. She herself lives in a little room in the garden during the summer. Her husband died a few years ago and is buried in the garden under some trees; they and the grave are railed off and kept locked.

Mme Lassalle also had a companion: 'There is such a famous dog here . . . very gentle and quiet. He wanders about the garden and tries to make friends with us. He is one of the Pyrenean dogs'.

There is no firm evidence of how Jones found the Chalet Lassalle, probably through contacts made in Pau such as Farnham Maxwell Lyte, but it is clear that he was very happy with their new situation, as he told Mr Badcock (one of the SANHS secretaries) in Taunton:

8.12: The view south from the site of the Chalet Lassalle at Vieuzac towards the valleys leading to Gavarnie (in the centre) and Cauterets (on the right). The development on the plain in the foreground came after Jones's visit. (AC)

We are enjoying our sojourn here greatly, though the heat at times is intense. Our house is perched high upon the slopes of the valley surrounded with vineyards and groves of Chestnut and Walnut. High mountains with precipitous sides tower behind us and from our windows and the terrace in front we have a full view of the gorges of Luz and Cauterets and of the mountain tops always covered with snow which form the boundaries of Spain. The valley of Argillez is one of the most fertile and luxuriant and presents a startling contrast with the bare and rocky mountain heights beyond. My boys occupy a tower (a part of the house) which belonged to Edward the Black Prince . . .[136]

Edward, the Black Prince (1330-1376), was the eldest son of Edward III. In 1362 he was made prince of Aquitaine and its virtually independent ruler, and therefore had control over this part of the Pyrenees. Two miles to the south of Argelès, in the village of Arcizans-Avant, is the Château du Prince Noir, although whether he ever lived either there or in the Chalet Lassalle is debatable. Places associated with the Black Prince seem to be the Aquitaine equivalent of beds in which Elizabeth I is said to have slept.

Most of Chalet Lassalle was pulled down shortly after the Jones's stay and the part of the site directly overlooking the newer areas of the town is now occupied by a retirement home, all that remains of the original house being the tall mediaeval square stone tower typical of the area. No good illustrations of the house have been found but a detailed description given by Arthur's eldest daughter Margaret, in a diary she entitled 'Three months in a French country house', shows that it was full of character; see Appendix 5 for the complete diary entry.

The family spent three months in Argelès, spending their time walking, studying the local nature and sightseeing. Margaret also spent some time in the spa town of Cauterets higher up the valley where she took the waters for the sake of her health benefits. Their presence in Argelès aroused some curiosity among the locals, one event in particular: 'The

8.13: La Tour de Vieuzac. The Chalet Lassalle was demolished and replaced by the Maison de Retraite on the right of the picture. (AC)

girls have manufactured a flag with the arms of the Prince duly blazoned which has been hoisted several times to the great amazement and at first the no small discomfiture of the gendarmes, who had some lurking suspicion of treason and insurrection'.[137]

Jones found much of historical and archaeological interest in the area which is noted for many fine churches and castles. He said, in a letter to Badcock in Taunton, that their condition was often poor, a fact that he attributed to the general poverty of the area: 'Here in the midst of the mountains there is little money to spare, and people's habits are more simple and primitive'.[138] However, things were looking up and M. Fould, a former government minister, had bought and was repairing the castle of Beaucens on the other side of the valley.[139]

At the beginning of August Jones visited the church of St André at Luz higher up the valley towards Gavarnie. In the nineteenth century the town became associated with the spa resort of St Sauveur on the opposite side of the valley but Luz had a much longer history. The church had been built in the twelfth century and fortified two hundred years later by the Knights Hospitallers of the Order of St John of Jerusalem; it is noted for carvings and inscriptions. Jones spent two hours taking rubbings that he intended to bring back for SANHS but they do not seem to have survived.

Jones also had a specific commission from William Sanford who at that time was working on his study of the *Felis* species. Sanford was interested in skeletons and asked Jones to make enquiries and if possible obtain specimens. It was not an easy task and it is not known if he was successful. A letter to Sanford on 1 July suggests that he was not too optimistic:

8.14: The Templar church at Luz. (Sheila Rabson)

I have been making enquiries about skeletons here but there are great difficulties. Whenever an izard is taken the <u>hotel-keepers</u> pounce upon it at once and you know that the French style of carving cannot fail to be fatal to your purposes. The <u>heads may</u> be had, mounted or as skeletons, but the whole frame of any of these not without incurring a great outlay I fear. I am going to Luz in a few days and will then make further enquiries, and if they are to be had at any reasonable charge I shall be delighted to fulfil your commission. Bears are becoming very scarce, as they are caught only in winter when driven down by hunger into the lowlands. We are keeping our eyes open on the <u>river</u>-side but as yet have seen no signs of the 'desman'. I saw one in the museum at Tarbes, and have asked Mr. Lyte and Mr Frossard at Bagnères de Bigorre to secure one for you if possible. [140]

The party's walking expeditions were quite challenging, particularly as they did not have the benefit of today's outdoor clothing and equipment. Walks to the top of quite difficult peaks, often in the company of a local guide, necessitated starting at a very early hour. In early July they went to Gavarnie, as Edith told her mother:

> . . . having secured rooms and ordered our dinner at the inn at Gavarnie we set out on foot for the celebrated 'Cirque'. It is 3 miles from the village and the gorge there comes to an abrupt end with a wall of rock, it is as the name expresses a <u>circle</u>. Over this from a tremendous height is a waterfall, the highest in the world, Mr. Packe says. [141] Altogether it is a very grand striking spot: the mountains towering above and around you and the water dashing down, as it seems almost from the sky. Much to our delight we found large patches of <u>snow</u> in the cirque! (the rocks round being so high the sun shines there only for a very short time so that last winter's snow is not yet melted) and we were able to walk on and eat some of it and that was on July 8th. Sarah and I found numbers of new flowers and I got some stones for Papa. We returned to dinner at 5 and as we had had nothing since breakfast at 8.30 we were all able to do full justice to it!

On the following day they climbed Le Piméné, one of the peaks surrounding the Cirque de Gavarnie:'

> After dinner Sarah and I had our flowers to arrange, the gentlemen took a stroll, and we all went to bed very early as we intended to get up at four the next morning to make the ascent of the Piméné, a mountain 9,300 ft about above the level of the sea, and 4 or 5,000 above Gavarnie. Fortunately we all woke or were called in time, we breakfasted at 4.30 and were off with our alpine stocks and guide at 5. During dressing I saw one of the most gorgeous effects I ever remember. The sun rose over the mountain behind the inn and shed such a beautiful bright golden light over the mountains in front of my window. I called Sarah but the gentlemen did not see it which was a pity. I suspect they were not awake enough! It was a perfect morning clear blue sky and the views were magnificent; starting so early everything was very fresh and pleasant and though part of the way it was hard walking yet we reached the highest point without over much fatigue in 3¾ hours. And <u>such</u> a view we had, grand beyond measure! Snow-capped peaks all round us as far as we could see and glaciers and sharp rocks and everywhere the beautiful clear sunlight.

They stayed at the Hôtel des Voyageurs in Gavarnie where 'our dinners were cooked every day by his worshipful the Mayor, the landlord of the Hôtel des Voyageurs, a patriarchal establishment in which there were living together several members of <u>three</u> generations!'.

Wildlife of the Pyrenees

The variety of habitats found in the Pyrenees – mountains, upland forests and meadows, rivers and lakes – supports a rich flora and fauna. Jones's papers make particular reference to the following.

8.15: Dog's Tooth Violet (*Erythronium dens canis*) the only erythronium species found in the wild in Europe.

8.16: Least Adder's Tongue (*Aphroglossum lusitanicum* or *Ophioglossum lusitanicum*): a small fern native in Europe on the western seaboard.

8.17: The Desman (*Galemys pyrenaicus*): a rare aquatic mammal that is also nocturnal and therefore extremely difficult to see. The mole is its closest cousin.

8.18: The Isard (*Rupicapra pyrenaica*): a Pyrenean mountain goat, similar to a chamois.

8.19: Footprints of the Pyrenean Wild Bear. The Pyrenean brown bear (*Ursus arctos arctos*): even rarer today than in the 1860s. With the killing of the last female in 2006 the species would have been heading for extinction in the Pyrenees if it were not for the recent, albeit controversial, introduction of bears from Slovenia.

8.20: The Alpine marmot (*Marmota marmota*): although now common in the Pyrenees it was reintroduced to the mountains only in 1948 and was not present in Jones's time there. The specimen brought back to England in 1868, as noted in John Jones's memoir, came from the Alps.

(Sources of images: 8.16 - Natura.pblogs.gr. 8.15, 8.17, 8.18, 8.20 - Parc National des Pyrénées/ J. Cédet; J.P.Crampe; A. Riffaud; Ch. Verdier.)

The Pyrenees in old postcards

8.21: La Cirque de Gavarnie. (AC)

8.22: Le Chaos de Gavarnie. (AC)

8.23: 'Crossing the Gave'. (AC)

8.24 *Les Montagnardes* – mountain guides. (AC)

Left: 8.25 The Pont Napoleon, Luz-St Sauveur. (AC)

Above. 8.26: *Une grimpade en Montagne.* Note the dress of the women climbers. (AC)

8.27: The square at St Savin, near Argelès-Gazost. (AC)

The Société Ramond

The Hôtel des Voyageurs at Gavarnie, sadly destroyed by fire in 2006, was more than just a local inn as it played an important role in the development of what has become known as 'Pyrénéeisme'. Interest in the many facets of the Pyrenees had been growing, and on 19 August 1864 the idea of setting up an organisation to promote the scientific study of the mountains was discussed at the hotel by three men, Farnham Maxwell Lyte, Charles Packe and Henry Russell. A few days later, at Bagnères-de-Bigorre, the Société Ramond was formally established and named after Ramond de Carbonnières (see page 53). Lyte became vice-president, Russell the secretary and Packe the deputy secretary. They were joined by Emilien Frossard of Bagnères, who took on the role of president. Lyte, Packe and Russell were all members of the Alpine Club of London, which might have inspired them to set up the society. However a comparison with SANHS is interesting and one wonders if the contact Lyte had with the former in 1856 had any influence in the establishment of the French society. The aims of the two bodies are generally similar although exploration has a specific place in the French body:

> *La Société a pour but l'étude de la chaîne Pyrénéenne, soit au point de vue scientifique, soit au point de vue des explorations proprement dites.*
> (Translated as, The Society has as its aim the study of the Pyrenees, from the point of view of both science and true exploration).

The membership of the French society was limited, initially at least, to 50 whereas SANHS in 1850 had 339 members. Clergymen played a much greater role in SANHS in the early days – one third of the members – whereas of the 42 members of the Société Ramond in 1867 only 5 were men of the cloth, namely three Frossards and two expatriate Anglicans (the Revd M. Heath from Bagnères and the Revd W. Webster from Biarritz). Both organisations had corresponding or honorary members who were often academics. It is also worth noting that men of a Protestant conviction played a dominant role; of the four founder members only Russell was a Catholic, and the point was made sixty years later that *'L'admiration de la montagne est une invention du protestantisme'.*[142] Emilien Frossard was the only founder member who was a minister of religion; he summed up very well how he saw the connection between studies of the natural world and religious belief in a way that Jones would have no

8.28: L'Hôtel des Voyageurs, Gavarnie - Lithographie de Jacottet, 1837. (*Revue des Pyrénées*)

doubt concurred:

> *Après l'étude de Dieu et du coeur humain, la contemplation de la nature dans ses magnifiques aspects peut etre considéréé comme l'une de nos plus douces jouissances, et l'un de nos devoirs les plus saints.*
> (Translated as, After the study of God and of the human heart the contemplation of nature in its magnificent aspects can be considered one of our sweetest pleasures and one of our most holy duties).

Of the founder members of the Société Ramond Farnham Maxwell Lyte has already been mentioned. Emilien Frossard had much in common with Arthur Jones. He was a French Protestant minister from Bagnères-de-Bigorre with an interest in geology who also had connections with England. He had lived there for some time and had married an English woman, Isabelle Trye, in Bath in 1826. His grandson, Emilien, later came to Somerset where, for forty years in the early twentieth century, he was the much-respected doctor in Bishops Lydeard: on his death he was buried in the village churchyard. Charles Packe was an Englishman, 'a botanist by passion and a lawyer by profession' and the author of the definitive *Guide to the Pyrenees,* first published in 1862. Henry Russell was a Franco-Irish count who was the most idiosyncratic of the four. In 1889 he purchased a lease of Le Vignemale, the highest peak in the French Pyrenees, where refuges were created high up near the summit for himself, his servants and his visitors. Jones certainly met Frossard, Lyte and Packe and became particularly associated with the first two. He also met another distinguished academic, Jules-Emile Planchon, a botanist who was head of the Department of Botanical Sciences at Montpellier University. However, it was with Frossard that Jones was able to pursue his geological interests, especially in the field of glacial studies.

The Glaciers of the High Pyrenees

A major influence on the landscape of the Pyrenees was the glaciation that took place in the Quaternary period, between 200,000 and 20,000 years ago. The scientific importance of this is reflected in the contents of the *Bulletin de la Société Ramond* which, between the Society's foundation and the end of the nineteenth century, contained 19 papers on the subject. The valley of the Gave de Pau, from its source at the Cirque de Gavarnie to the terminal moraine just to the north of Lourdes, together with its tributary valleys, was of particular interest and Jones became involved in a major study that was being carried out. The researchers were two other members of the Société Ramond, Dr Charles Martins (Professor in the Faculty of Medicine at the University of Montpellier) and Edouard Collomb (a member of the Société Géologique de France, from Paris). The work had already started and Dr Martins had reported to a *séance* (a meeting) of the Société Ramond on 25 October 1866 on a study he had just made of glaciation in the valley at Lourdes. The research by Martins and Collomb was published in 1868 by the Société Géologique de France under the title of *Essai sur l'ancien glacier de la vallée d'Argelès.* A copy in the SANHS library, annotated with the words 'Sommersetshire archaeological and natural history society from the author', was possibly brought home by Arthur Jones.[143]

8.29: Emilien Frossard. (Wikipedia)

8.30: The cover of the paper or *essai* by Collomb and Martins. (SANHS)

Until the nineteenth century the idea that ice could have been responsible for the development of landforms was regarded at best as unlikely and at worst contrary to biblical teaching. The definitive work propounding new evidence on the role of glaciers was published in 1840 by the Swiss naturalist Louis Agassiz.[144] In October 1840, while Jones was at Glasgow University, Agassiz visited the city for a meeting of the British Association for the Advancement of Science. While there is no reference in Jones's diary to his hearing about this he must have been aware of it. One can also assume that Jones would have been present, nineteen years later, on 14 November 1859, to hear William Sanford's account of his visit to the Aår glacier in Switzerland in the company of Louis Agassiz, or at least have seen the verbatim report in the local paper.

Jones would have welcomed the opportunity to be involved in Martins and Collomb's research. Their paper shows that he contributed in particular to studies of the area around Argelès and, in co-operation with Emilien Frossard, used fossil identification to trace the origin of glacial erratics. Jones's experience and knowledge of the Devonian rocks in England would have been of help and Frossard was also particularly interested, being a prolific author on geology for the Société Ramond's *Bulletin*. Jones had accompanied Martins up the mountainside just to the south of Argelès, known as Escorne-Crabe, to look at a lateral moraine at a height of 1969-2363ft above the Gave de Pau; the visit was recorded in Martin and Collomb's paper:

> *Un de nous a étudie plus specialement l'extremité meridionale de cette moraine, au-dessus du village d'Arcizans, en compagnie de M. Arthur Jones de Taunton, écclesiastique anglais qui habitait alors Argelès.*
> *De ce point, je constatai a l'aide de mon niveau que le pic de Gez (altitude 1097 metres), qui domine Argelès, est entièrement couvert de blocs erratiques, et M. Arthur Jones s'est assuré depuis qu'ils étaient egalement granitiques.*

Translated as 'One of us had studied especially the southern extremity of this moraine, above the village of Arcizans, in the company of Mr. Arthur Jones of Taunton, an English (*sic*) clergyman who was living in Argelès. From this point I established with the help of my level that the Pic de Gez (1097 m, 3600 ft) which dominates Argelès, is entirely covered with erratic blocks, and Mr Arthur Jones has assured himself since that they are likewise granitic'. Jones's great help in identifying the age and origin of glacial erratics was noted; with Frossard he had found scattered near Argelès fragments of rock, most notably Devonian schistes with *Reptora reticularis,* which originated from the neighbourhood of Gavarnie and Gèdre

Fig.12 - Bloc erratique de granite
reposant sur des schistes crétacés
dans un bois de chènes et de chataigniers, près Lourdes
longueur 9ᵐ.50 largeur 7ᵐ.40 hauteur 2ᵐ.60.

8.31: A glacial erratic at Mont Gez, near Argelès from a sketch in Collomb & Martin. (SANHS)

Montpellier

Towards the end of September Jones and his family, without his niece Edith who had returned to England in July, left Argelès for the university town of Montpellier, possibly at the suggestion of M. Planchon. Jones had enjoyed his time in the mountains and recommended the benefits of 'perfect and absolute rest' to William Sanford, but as he said to him in a letter on 1 July 1867:

> My rest, however has been chiefly a <u>change</u> of occupation, for you may suppose I have too long been used to <u>work</u> to find pleasure in absolute idleness. I am, however, sometimes longing to return, and to work for the Institutions at home in which I am still interested.[145]

He did have some unfinished business in the Pyrenees: 'I have not forgotten your commission [for skeletons] and still hope to be able to carry out your wishes in part at least, though it is very difficult just now to lay hold upon anything. The visitors at the watering places take all'. However he may have been partly successful, as John Jones recorded in his memoire: 'In a stream father secured a 'desmond rat' a sort of vole with long snout and very rare. He got it stuffed by Arthur [his eldest surviving son] and put it in Taunton museum after our return'.

Working with Martins made quite an impression on Jones:

8.32: The Argelès valley as it might have appeared at the time of the Quaternary glaciation (from a watercolour by unknown artist, but possibly Emilien Frossard). (SANHS)

> In about three weeks time we shall be on our way to Montpellier, where in all probability we shall pass the winter. A few weeks since I made the acquaintance of Prof. C. Martins here and accompanied him in his geological survey. He is completing his observations on the moraines and erratic blocks so associated with the ancient glaciers of the Pyrenees. This has added greatly to the interest and pleasure of my rambles here. He holds the chair of Nat. Hist. at Montpellier and I am looking forward much to the pleasure of renewing his acquaintance.

Jones planned to spend the winter in Montpellier and hoped to renew his acquaintance with the academics he had met in the Pyrenees. The family took up residence at the Villa Marie, a small villa in the Chemin de Castelnau, on the northern outskirts of the town. They made the acquaintance of the local Protestant community and the boys attended local schools. In addition to studies of music and drawing the three eldest girls were also kept busy with courses of lectures almost every day, given by different professors and expressly for young ladies, on history, literature, physiology, arithmetic and geometry and natural philosophy.[146]

He did keep in touch with his academic contacts in Montpellier but also went further afield. At the beginning of February 1868, armed with letters of introduction from 'some of the principal professors here', he took a trip through the Midi via Narbonne and Carcassonne to Toulouse. At Narbonne he visited the museum, where he found the human remains of great interest, and made notes about the cathedral.[147] Although it is not mentioned in his letter to Sanford, Jones would have been at Carcassonne during the fifty year long reconstruction of the mediaeval citadel by the French architect Viollet le Duc.

It was at Toulouse that he made his best contact on this trip. Edouard Filhol was Directeur of the College of Medicine, mayor of the town and a person of great influence there. He was also a member of the Société Ramond and 'one of a very few men of eminence I have met in France who does not understand English, so I should advise you to write to him in French'. Filhol was greatly interested in fossils and took Jones over the Museum of Natural History, which was especially rich in <u>Cane</u> bones. Jones saw distinct advantages in sharing information and even specimens, as he told Sanford:

> I thought you would be interested to communicate with M. Filhol, and he expressed himself very anxious to compare notes with you especially in the *Felis Speleca* [?] which is his special study. I promised to write to you and to give you his address. They would be very glad to effect <u>exchanges</u> with us. I did not myself feel justified to make any offer or promise, leaving it entirely with you who know the Collection so much better than I do. I confess myself rather reluctant to part with any specimens not most clearly and obviously duplicates or triplicates. They are <u>very</u> poor in *Hydras*, and *Felis* and *Elephas* at Toulouse but especially rich in bears. By the same post I send you a brochure on the bears by Mr. Trutah (excluding one plate […] size) which may interest you if you have begun the bears. You had better keep it until our return. I had asked Bidgood for a set of the 'Felis' plates he had finished in the spring which I am about to send to M. Filhol. I think they will send me some specimens to bring home with me for our museum. I also left them a copy of our last vol. and they promised me the catalogue of their cave fossils when it is published for our society.[148]

Whether this letter was followed up with further contact between Taunton and Toulouse is not known, but it does raise the question of the language used by English visitors to this part of France. The geography of language in nineteenth century France has been brilliantly described by Graham Robb in his book *The Discovery of France*.[149] 'Metropolitan' French was used by the court, government and intellectuals and many people at that level would have had some facility in English. At the same time many of their counterparts in England could converse in French and it would not be surprising to find that Jones and Sanford were among them. However, the common language in the south west of France at this time was Gascon, a variety of Langue d'Oc, and in the valleys of the central Pyrenees the situation was made even more complicated by the use of dialects, which could vary from one valley to the next. Robb comments that in 1858 the Virgin Mary would have spoken to Bernadette Soubirous in the local dialect of Lourdes! These local tongues would be used for everyday purposes by the people with whom the English visitors came into contact, such as tradesman, servants and mountain guides, but no doubt people 'got by' and the ability to communicate would have improved on both sides as the century progressed.

Jones's aim was to make the most of the educational advantages of Montpellier and then return to England at the end of May 1868, but the attractions of the town must have been strong as the family remained a little longer. However, their stay was marked by a yet another family tragedy when on 15 June his third daughter Mary died, aged 15. She was buried in the town, spurring the family to return to England.

A note about Money

To conclude the story of Arthur Jones's time in the south of France, this is the appropriate place to reflect on how he supported his large family while out of the country, having resigned from his position at the Taunton chapel in February 1867. It has already been noted that the chapel paid him an annual salary of £180. His account books show that in the period leading up to his Pyrenees visit his income included, in addition to this sum, considerable investment income and regular payments from other sources such as his Blake relatives. His first wife Mary left him £2,000 in 1842, but most of his money came from the settlement on his marriage with Margaret Blake, dated 31 December 1845. The sum of £8947 17s was invested in 3% Consols in the names of William Blake and his brother-in-law Edward Jarman.; in April 1856 Jarman was replaced by another brother-in-law, the Revd John Robberds. The investment was allocated in three ways: £1,000 to Arthur; and of the balance of £7,947 17s the 'first moiety' (*i.e.* half) in trust to his children and the 'second moiety' in trust to him. Specific investment interest first appears on 21 January 1857, the £8,947 17s Consols giving a dividend of £125 5s 5d.

By the time Jones went to the Pyrenees his investments had grown to about £13,000 (approximately £600,000 in today's value),[150] helped by £1,000 from the estate of Edward Jarman, who had died in April 1866. In April 1867 Jones received £444 7s 6d from the sale of investments, and at the beginning of 1868 the sum of £587 8s 6d from the estate of William Baker, a previous SANHS secretary. While in the south of France he made regular (monthly or two monthly) withdrawals of £100 to £150, presumably for everyday living expenses. On 23 March 1867 Miss Hollins received a payment of £15 at the end of her employment as the family's governess.

8.33: Extract from Jones's note book, showing entries for his expenditure during his Pyrenean visit. (BA)

Chapter Nine
The Return to Taunton

THE JONES PARTY did not come straight back to England. From Montpellier they travelled up the Rhone valley to Geneva, spending a day or so on the way at Arles, Avignon and Chambery. From Geneva they took a lake steamer to Château Chillon where they stayed for some weeks in a pension just above the castle, moving on to Champéry near the Dents du Midi. Their time was spent exploring and one of the boys, Arthur, acquired a marmot which he brought back to England, presumably not alive. From Champéry the journey took them via Berne, Interlaken and Lake Lucerne to Basel, then to Heidelberg by a Rhine steamer, and on to Ostend, Dover and thence back to Somerset.[151]

On their return to England the family stayed at first with their Blake relatives at Bridge House near South Petherton. Situated on the south side of the Fosse Way (today the A303 where it crosses the River Parrett) this large family home was built in 1859, but survived for only 100 years.[152] From Bridge House they moved to 3 The Crescent in Taunton, part of an elegant terrace overlooking a green space now occupied by County Hall. It was described by John Jones as 'a somewhat old-fashioned but comfortable house of red brick and west of town with large comfortable rooms, three stories and a basement, walled garden about 100ft long flower bed all round, bit of lawn, door at end leading to a back lane'.[153] In the summer of 1869 the family spent several weeks at Porlock Weir before moving to Tauntfield, a large house off South Road, where Jones was to spend the rest of his life.

Arthur Jones rejoined the congregation at the Mary Street chapel but not as the

9.1: Bridge House, South Petherton, home of the Blake family. (BA)

9.2: 3 The Crescent, Taunton, where Jones stayed on his return from France. Part of a Grade 2* listed terrace built in 1807. It is now occupied by offices. (AC)

minister. He had resigned from his post in February 1867 and there was a new man in charge. He dropped the title of 'Reverend', as he explained to William Sanford in June 1869: 'During the time I was engaged in the <u>active</u> duties of the Ministry I always expected the <u>prefix</u>, not for my <u>own</u> but for my <u>office</u> sake. Now that to all practical purposes I am become more than half a layman I am quite indifferent'.[154] He did, however, resume his duties as secretary to SANHS at a time when important decisions were becoming necessary, especially in respect of the museum collections.

SANHS welcomed Jones's return, as during his absence the organisation had had some difficulties. It was obliged to find a *locum tenens* for him while he was abroad and to compound the problem the other two secretaries had resigned. He was aware of this through his correspondence with Sanford, writing on 1 July from Argelès-de-Bigorre:

> I am sorry to find the Archaeological is absolutely without a Secretary. I wonder at Mr. Brown's giving up. It would have done Mr. Elliot a world of good if he had buckled to and done himself what work there was to be done. What I am most afraid of is that unless an <u>Executive</u> can be found at Taunton the headquarters of the Society may be moved elsewhere.[155]

The pattern of SANHS events continued with meetings, *conversazioni* and visits to places of interest. As before Jones provided papers to meetings as well as organising visits and contributing to the *Proceedings*. On one occasion at least, his personal activities led to a degree of dissatisfaction among his colleagues. In 1869, a visit to the Mendip Hills in the north of Somerset was proposed, in respect of which Jones had written to Sanford on 15 June. He gave details of the visit 'which would not be complete if we do not visit the Caverns and have an exposition of the cave bone'.[156] One of the excursions would be from Axbridge to Rowberrow, Dolbury Camp, Burrington church, Combe and caves, and over the Mendip to Cheddar Gorge. Jones had a curious question about Burrington Cave: 'Is it accessible to ladies? I mean the ordinary run of women'; 'ordinary' perhaps in contrast to his daughters and his niece who had undertaken challenging ascents in the Pyrenees. His letter ended by saying that he would be going to Porlock Weir on 17 June and hoped the arrangements would be in place by then. However, on 29 June

9.3: Tauntfield, South Road, Taunton, where Jones stayed from 1870 until his death. (AC)

William Hunt, the local secretary in Bristol, wrote to Sanford (presumably) that 'as I have had the bother of arranging our meeting this year I am very anxious that it should go off well'; he adds that 'Jones will stay in Porlock wh[ich] has occasioned no little letter writing'.[157] Jones told William Blake that he had 'engaged the Porlock Weir Cottage for 7 or 8 weeks from June 18th or 23rd. We are all very pleased to look forward to it'.[158]

Jones was concerned about the direction in which SANHS was going. At the 1871 Annual Meeting, in Crewkerne, E.A. Freeman gave a paper on its role and scope. At the evening meeting Jones 'expressed his regret that papers on Natural History had been crowded out. He had proposed a paper on the geology of Crewkerne and its neighbourhood, but there was no time to read it. He thought that some arrangement should be made for devoting a second day to the reading of papers'.[159] At this time the Society was also caught up in the development of a national approach to conservation. At the 23rd Annual Meeting, in Wincanton on 23 August 1870, Jones reported on representations that had been made to the Secretary of State about the conservation of ancient monuments. By the meeting in Taunton a year later it had been agreed to set up a committee to co-operate with the promoters of a legislative measure for the protection and preservation of historical monuments. A list of the more interesting objects in the county was prepared and Jones accompanied Mr F.H. Dickinson, another senior member of the Society, to a meeting with John Lubbock, the MP for Maidstone who had a great interest in scientific matters, with the view of furthering the matter.[160] A Bill was to be presented in Parliament in the next session, but legal protection for ancient monuments was not achieved until 1882 after several failed attempts.

Chapter Ten
Civic Activities

AS IN MOST TOWNS IN THE NINETEENTH CENTURY Taunton's rapid growth was accompanied by the establishment of civic institutions to meet the needs of the population. Clergymen of all denominations often played a leading role in these bodies and in promoting the social as well as the spiritual well-being of the inhabitants: indeed many saw no distinction between the two. Prominent among these clergymen was the vicar of Holy Trinity Church, the Revd Frederick Jeremiah Smith, a man of wealth and described by a recent author as 'that superbly bigoted philanthropist'.[161] Smith failed in his attempt to become the first chairman of the Taunton Board of Health when it was set up in 1849 but went on to make his mark in the town, providing funds for two churches, St John the Baptist on Park Street and St Andrew at Rowbarton. At the same time Jones's predecessor at the Mary Street chapel, Robert Montgomery, actively encouraged his congregation to play their part in the life of the town in various ways and was personally involved in wider initiatives. He was an active member of the 'British Unitarians against Slavery' movement and after handing over to Jones went to America in the summer of 1852 to pursue its campaign there.

Jones's interest in civic matters had begun in Glasgow with his membership of the Liberal Association. In Northampton and Bridgwater he had joined local organisations, and before he left for the Pyrenees he had already become involved in such activities in Taunton. On his return, partly perhaps because he had no duties at the chapel to take up his time, he became even more involved, often at an influential level. This involvement was so great that when reporting in the autumn of 1873 a proposal to establish a memorial to him the *Taunton Courier* commented that 'No man in this place, probably, during the last twenty years, has contributed more efficiently to those local institutions which mark the higher civilisation of a town'.[162] Like many of his contemporaries in mid-Victorian England Jones took an optimistic and positive view of progress and of the role of Christianity, as expressed in the conclusion to his first paper to SANHS in 1853, albeit tempered with a nostalgia for a world which was fast disappearing. He believed that progress was divinely ordained:

> Through the advancement of civilisation and the elevating influence of the Christian faith, great and happy changes have been brought about in the character and aspect of society since the period of which this paper treats. The descendants of the Celt and the Saxon, instead of waging deadly war against each other, are merged into one people, enjoying in common the blessings of their common social and political privileges.
> Much as we rejoice in these changes in the aspect of society, I confess, nevertheless, that while looking down from the heights, upon the plains through which the muddy Parrett now flows, I have sometimes wished the aspect of the country had not changed; and that we could still stand upon the VOEL-DEN [*i.e. The Polden Hills*], gazing on the expanding estuaries on either side, glistening in the sunlight beneath our feet, and watch the white sails gliding from their entrance at Combwich, to their ancient destination at Llongborth.
> Yet we feel that in the changes of the world there is progress. The beautiful often gives way to the useful. Cornfields rise with their golden harvest from the depths of the waters. We bow to a higher power; we acknowledge and revere the Supreme wisdom of Him, who overrules the affairs of men.[163]

A brief survey of his activities shows that he had broad interests but had played a particular role in education in its widest sense. Probably his most important initiative came in 1856 when he founded the Taunton School of Science and Art: he stayed actively involved, being its joint honorary secretary until his death. He took a broad view of what should be studied at the school. At the prize giving in August 1857 he gave 'a long and able address', to which his large audience frequently responded with cheers, as fully reported in the *Somerset County Gazette*. The school had an economic and social as well as artistic purpose:

> Their chief object in establishing the school was to provide for the artizans of Taunton such art instruction as should enable them to compete with the manufacturers of works of art; to elevate their tastes and keep them from debasing pursuits, and to advance them in their various callings. [Mr Jones] had a strong impression that blacksmiths, carpenters, builders, masons, and others should learn drawing if they would excel as workmen.[164]

Although initially the school covered both arts and sciences the latter were dropped from its title. It moved into the Mechanic's Institute in Bath Place where it stayed until 1889 when it transferred to the Victoria Rooms on the Parade. Its Bath Place home is now marked by a blue plaque. In 1907 it relocated again to new buildings in Corporation Street. It was a direct ancestor of the present Somerset College of Arts and Technology. Jones was especially concerned with the Taunton College School, originally established as a free grammar school by Bishop Fox in 1522, which after a long period of uncertainty,

10.1: Taunton College School, 1827 (from a painting by J.C. Buckler (SANHS))

had been re-established in 1855. Arthur's sons were pupils at the school. Using historical evidence about the original purposes of the school he successfully persuaded the Charity Commissioners in 1858 that pupils who were children of Dissenters should not be required to learn the catechism of the Church of England.[165]

In 1854 a Mutual Improvement Class had been formed at the Mechanics Institute in Bath Place in Taunton, under the presidency of Jones and the Revd H. Addicott, for the purposes of critical readings, discussions and essays. In November of the next year a Taunton Industrial Exhibition was held in the Great Hall at Taunton Castle; as well as being a patron and a member of the organising committee Jones exhibited an African gourd, a flask, sandals, a comb, a pillar and two ancient records.[166]

10.2: Memorial plaque in Bath Place, Taunton. (AC)

Jones was also secretary of the local committee of the Oxford examinations syndicate, chairman of the proprietors of the Taunton Institution and chairman of the Management Committee of the Taunton and Somerset Hospital; the last of these positions he held until his death. He qualified as a Justice of the Peace at the Spring Sessions in Wells in 1871, and when sitting on the bench was not the typical image of a Victorian magistrate: 'He always displayed a kindly bearing when in the court, towards those appearing before him'.[167]

There was also talk of his standing for parliament. From his time at Glasgow University, and possibly before, he had been interested in politics, although not always actively. His letters give an occasional insight into his political feelings, as in 1867 when he commented to Badcock about universal suffrage in France: 'I do not know what the extension of the suffrage may do in England but I earnestly hope it may not prove so destructive of liberty and freedom as the so-called universal suffrage in France. But our English men are made of better stuff I believe'.[168]

It is not clear what Jones meant by this comment. There had been universal suffrage (for men only) in France since 1848, but under the Second Empire (1852-1870) of Louis Napoleon its effectiveness was severely constrained by, among other things, control of the press, the forbidding of free speech and gerrymandering. Britain was behind France in the extension of the right to vote; the Great Reform Act of 1832 provided a standard franchise of £10 householders in towns, while in the country some leaseholders were included as well as freeholders, but it was not until 1884 that the right to vote was given to most adult men. There was an intermediate Act in 1867 and it might be that Jones felt that in Britain progress was being made despite its late start, whereas across the Channel men were not resisting strongly enough the forces of repression. Jones became more politically active in Taunton after his return from the Pyrenees. On 19 December 1870 he chaired, as President, the annual meeting of the Taunton Working Men's Liberal Association at the Parade Assembly Rooms, expounding his Liberal views with some force in his address to the meeting. His last public speech was to the Association in December 1872, held in the chief room at the Town Hall, which was 'well filled' for the occasion.[169]

In November 1857 there came an opportunity for Jones to put his geological knowledge to practical rather than merely academic use, when the *Somerset County Gazette* carried an advertisement proposing the establishment of a Taunton Waterworks Company.[170] It was becoming recognised that a comprehensive approach to the supply of water for the people of Taunton was desirable, although it is interesting that initially the case concentrated on the need to reduce the hardness of the water available to residents rather than on public health considerations. The proposal included a provisional list of directors and a statement of the case for a public water supply, supported by chemical analysis of possible sources. It stimulated considerable discussion about the need for the new system and its cost, and questions about the suitability of the source above the village of Blagdon on the scarp slope of the Blackdown Hills just to the south of Taunton. The advertisement prompted a response from Jones in the *County Gazette* on 5 December in which he lay before the paper's readers 'a brief statement of what appears to me to be the real state of the matter, especially as it bears upon the objects and purposes of the Water-works Company'.[171] He supported the proposal with great satisfaction and outlined his conclusions on the quality and probable quantity of the 'article offered to (the consumers) by this company'. His contribution to the debate was based on his knowledge of the geology of the Blackdowns, and on his own chemical analysis: 'The application of the soap test, and other chemical tests, to the samples of water which I brought myself from the springs referred to in the prospectus did not enable me to detect any appreciable difference between it and rainwater'. As a result he became heavily involved in the company. He bought shares and was appointed a founding director in 1858. He stood down from its board between 1860 and 1866, probably because of family problems, and again in 1867 when he was in the south of France. On returning to England he rejoined the board, becoming vice-chairman then chairman, being re-appointed to the latter post in April 1873 just before his death.

Chapter Eleven
Arthur Jones's religious views

ARTHUR JONES'S RELIGIOUS VIEWS were inseparable from his scientific and antiquarian interests. In common with most other contributors he included a reference to God as Creator in many of his papers to the Society, as when discussing the geology around Dunster: 'The record is writ by the Almighty hand itself upon the rocky tablets of everlasting ages'.[172] Unitarianism, the path followed by Arthur and his brother John, had its roots in the religious dissent of the sixteenth century. It was part of the complex web of dissenting groups in the succeeding two centuries, with particular links to Presbyterianism, although the boundaries between different traditions seem to have been flexible. A simplistic definition of Unitarianism at that time is that its adherents accepted neither the doctrine of the Trinity nor the divinity of Christ, preferring to concentrate on the idea of a single God. However it was also marked by characteristics such as tolerance, refusal to be held to particular creeds and openness to new ideas, especially in scientific fields, while not disregarding the central importance of the Bible and the life and teachings of Jesus as a source of inspiration and guidance. The Heol Awst chapel in Carmarthen where Jones spent his childhood was not Unitarian but in the congregational tradition, with Trinitarian tendencies, an approach which led some Unitarians to move away and worship elsewhere in Carmarthen. However, the congregations which Arthur Jones served later did generally consider themselves Unitarian, although not necessarily under that name.

Jones certainly considered himself to be a 'Christian' but his public stance on matters of faith did sometimes give rise to controversy. At the end of January 1861 an event was held at the Mary Street chapel which included speeches on the present state of Unitarianism. A 'discourse' by Jones, printed in the *Somerset County Gazette* on 2 February, provoked letters from 'Enquirer', 'A Wayfaring Man', 'A Lay Churchman' and 'A Well-wisher', and finally a response from Jones on 16 March. Objections to Unitarianism had been put forward – it was negative, unimaginative and not in accordance with biblical teaching - which Jones was keen to refute. The debate in the *Somerset County Gazette* focussed on what view Jones held of the divinity of Christ, an argument not made easier by his statement that while rejecting the Athanasian Creed he had no problems in accepting the earlier Apostles' Creed, despite the fact that as a Unitarian he rejected the idea of holding to a particular creed. The difference between the two creeds is important [see Appendix 5 for the full text of both creeds from the 1662 Book of Common Prayer]. Both can be found in the Church of England's Book of Common Prayer: the Apostles Creed is in the service for both Morning and Evening Prayer while the Athanasian Creed is set instead of the Apostles Creed for major feast days and some saints days in Morning Prayer. The Athanasian Creed is much longer and more prescriptive, focussing on an exposition of the doctrine of the Trinity and ending with the strong statement that 'This is the Catholick Faith: which except a man believe faithfully, he cannot be saved'. The Apostles Creed is shorter and can be read as being not explicitly Trinitarian and therefore likely to be more acceptable to someone of Unitarian inclinations. Jones's position was not always clear: the *Somerset County Gazette* in its tribute to Jones in April 1873 commented that some people felt that towards the end of his life he was becoming more Trinitarian in his outlook,[173] a view strongly refuted by his brother-in-law the Revd John Robberds in the Unitarian newspaper *The Inquirer:* 'While identifying himself with the general interests of the town of his adoption, he remained steadfast to the form of religious faith of which he had so long been a preacher and a pastor', and in a letter to the newspaper.[174] However, a modern reader, unless trained in theology, might find the various arguments put forward by the opposing sides in the debate somewhat inconclusive if not confusing.

Whatever Arthur Jones's religious views might have been he did get on well with people of other traditions, both publicly and privately. In public his Unitarian approach was evident. As chairman of the hospital management committee he was keen that patients should have access to their own spiritual advisors whatever their denomination, and he was often seen attending lectures by speakers of other religious views.[175] In private it was the same. When Sarah Ellen, the first wife of his Anglican friend William Sanford, died in August 1867 Jones sent his condolences from the Pyrenees:

> I have not written to you earlier to convey to you the assurance of my sympathy and condolence because I was unwilling to intrude upon the sacredness of your sorrow. I know too well what the trial is through which you have passed. I know also how weak and powerless are all human words of comfort however well meant. There is but one source of true comfort – a living faith in His Words who brought life and immortality to light and a loving trust in that heavenly Father who ordains and sanctifies the events of our chequered life.[176]

On a more practical front, when Jones rented Silver Street House in South Road in Taunton in the 1850s and 60s he had much contact with the adjoining Roman Catholic convent. The house had been acquired by the convent in the 1830s to provide it with a source of income and the relations between the nuns and the Jones family were good, John Jones remembering later that 'the lady abbess [was] a great friend of father in spite of his being a Unitarian minister and consulted him frequently on business matters'.

11.1: The interior of the Heol Awst Chapel, Carmarthen, with the minister Revd J. Towyn Jones and the author. Typically for a Dissenters' chapel the provision for preaching takes centre stage (Sheila Rabson)

Chapter Twelve
Last Days

ON THE LAST DAY OF 1872 Arthur Jones wrote to his friend William Sanford to wish him well for the New Year, adding 'I have been under the doctor's care for some days – derangement of the digestive system. There are very few things as yet that I dare venture on in the way of meal-foods but I hope I have turned the corner. The attack has left me very weak'.[177] However despite the attention of several doctors, including Dr Kinglake and Mr Cornish of Taunton, the suggestion of treatment in London and another opinion from Dr Budd of Clifton, his condition worsened. His final days are recounted in letters from his eldest daughter Margaret to her Uncle William Blake.[178] Jones

12.1: The Jones family graves in the cemetery in Wellington Road, Taunton, including those of Jones and his second wife Margaret. They were originally surrounded by iron railings. (AC)

died at his home in Taunton on 23 April, a few days short of his 55th birthday.

The funeral took place on Monday 28 April at the Taunton cemetery on the Wellington road and not at the Mary Street chapel, perhaps because of the number of mourners expected. The *Taunton Courier* described the occasion:

> A large number of the townsmen assembled at the Fountain at the end of East Street, and joined in the mournful procession as it reached that point.
> Several private carriages followed the mourners from the residence of the deceased; most of the local magistrates taking part in this last token of respect to their late companion. The two borough members, Messrs Barclay and James, came down specially to attend the funeral, and returned to town immediately afterwards.
> The procession was augmented at various points, and the total number assembled at the cemetery was very considerable.
> The chapel was completely filled, and the service listened to with devout attention.
> The Rev. Mr Robberds, (of Cheltenham), a brother-in-law of the deceased officiated,

and after reading the beautiful chapter adopted in nearly every burial service by all sects and denominations, the rev. gentleman made a few affecting and appropriate remarks on the memory of him whom they had come to consign to the tomb....

On arriving at the grave, the mournful ceremony was concluded; the present minister of Mary street chapel (the Rev. J. Birks), and Dr Cornish, who attended the deceased during his last illness, standing together by the grave.

On the coffin were placed three wreaths of choice white flowers, and several bunches of flowers were also thrown into the grave by some of the female members of the Unitarian Chapel.[179]

The *Somerset County Gazette* gave more details: 'In most of the public offices, business establishments and private houses, blinds were drawn or shutters partially closed as a final mark of respect' while the bell at the parish church of St Mary Magdalen in the town centre tolled a knell during the progress of the funeral. The grave of Arthur Jones and his wife Margaret is marked by a simple tombstone, next to a similar stone in which the remains of other members of the Jones family, including his son Downing, had been interred. Originally they were guarded by an ornamental iron rail, which is no longer there. Jones's coffin was of polished oak with plain black iron furniture.[180]

In the obituary which John Robberds wrote for the *Inquirer*, the national Unitarian paper, he gave his assessment of his brother-in-law's qualities:

12.2: A photographic image thought to be the Revd John Robberds. (BA)

> The qualities which mainly enabled him to win his way to influential positions in his various relations, were judgment, tact, a courteous and conciliatory bearing, and excellent business habits. He had a natural gift of ingratiating himself with all whom he came in contact, which, however, was controlled and guided by a serious desire to promote, so far as in him lay, the interests of truth, freedom, charity, and the culture of literature, science and art.[181]

The responses in Taunton to Jones's passing reflected the esteem with which he was held in different sections of the community. The Taunton Courier began its report of the funeral by saying that 'the grave has now closed over the mortal remains of one who in his life time exercised no inconsiderable influence over much which concerned many of the public institutions connected with Taunton'. After rehearsing the various contributions he had made in the twenty years since he arrived in the town the paper went on to make a comment which suggests that he was not always recognised as part of the town's 'establishment': 'Differing though he did from us most materially, both in his political and religious views, we willingly close the doors of controversy in the presence of the dead, and cordially recognise the sincerity of the former and the breadth of the latter'.[182]

This hint of controversy was repeated when the question of a permanent monument to Jones arose. On 13 December 1873 a notice appeared in the *Somerset County Gazette* under the heading of 'The Jones Memorial' inviting subscriptions from 'those who desire to commemorate, independently of political objects, the various public services of the late Mr William Arthur Jones'. The sums collected would be put towards the founding of a scholarship or exhibition at Taunton College School to be named after him. The notice was placed by the High Sheriff, F.H. Dickinson, E.A. Freeman, Rev. W. Hunt, Col. Pinney, W.A. Sanford and W.E. Surtees, all members of SANHS, and a total of £35 had already been promised'.

THE JONES MEMORIAL.

THE UNDERMENTIONED GENTLEMEN have consented to act as a COMMITTEE for the application of SUBSCRIPTIONS, to be paid to the several Taunton Banks, by those who desire to commemorate, independently of political objects, the various public services of the late Mr. WILLIAM ARTHUR JONES :—

The HIGH SHERIFF OF THE COUNTY.
F. H. DICKINSON, Esq.
E. A. FREEMAN, Esq.
The Rev. W. HUNT.
Col. PINNEY.
W. A. SANFORD, Esq.
W. E. SURTEES, Esq.

It is the intention, in order to give permanence to the object of the subscription, to apply the sums collected to the FOUNDING OF A SCHOLARSHIP, or EXHIBITION, at the Taunton College School, to be named after Mr. JONES.

The following subscriptions have been already promised :

The Sheriff	£5	W. A. Sanford, Esq.,	£5
Lady Taunton	5	W. E. Surtees, Esq.,	5
F. H. Dickinson, Esq.	5	Henry Badcock, Esq.	3
W. Pinney, Esq.	5	Arthur Malet, Esq.	2

12.3: The notice proposing a memorial to Jones in the *Somerset County Gazette*, 13.12.1873. (SHC)

The notice elicited a response from 'TSP', one Thomas Penny, a prominent local businessman and Baptist, who objected to the proposed scholarship asking 'Was Mr Jones a Churchman?' and 'Did he take an interest in this above all other institutions in the town?'[183] A further letter, from 'A Churchman', also questioned the proposal on the grounds that it was not appropriate for someone who rejected the divinity of Christ to be commemorated at a school which had been established in accordance with Church of England teachings.[184] Mr Surtees submitted a response to these arguments.[185] Whether the proposal succeeded is not known, but in any case it would not have been a permanent memorial to Jones. The school had moved in 1870 to a site on South Road until 1879 when financial problems brought it eventually back to its former home where it struggled on, closing eventually in 1885.

SANHS's own recognition of Jones's contribution to its activities was more generous. At the Annual Meeting in Wells, on 19 August 1873, the President, William Sanford, paid tribute to his colleague and friend: 'Mr Jones, by his unremitting attention, by his considerable ability, by his genial manners and general kindness, had done very much for the society, and his death would be a heavy and perhaps an irreparable loss, for it would be difficult to replace him'. Jones's successor as secretary, the Revd W. Hunt, added his own tribute:

> To a more than ordinary knowledge on general and archaeological subjects, and a scientifically cultured mind, which rendered him one of the most valuable officers that this Society ever had, Mr Jones added a kindness of heart and amenity of manner which endeared him to all who had the pleasure of knowing him, and those who knew him best lament him most.[186]

Inevitably the idea arose of a permanent memorial being provided by the Society. After the Wells meeting P. King Meade King suggested to William Blake that it might take the form of a simple monument in the cemetery or, far better, a public drinking fountain in Taunton.[187] In the event a much more appropriate monument was chosen.

12.4: Jones's memorial stone outside the Museum of Somerset at Taunton Castle. (AC)

In 1873 the Society was in the process of buying Taunton Castle for use as a museum; the Castle had already been used for public events. The opportunity for the Society to acquire the property was brought to the attention of its committee in February 1873[188] and on 5 March a special meeting of the Society's Council resolved to pursue the purchase.[189] As part of the purchase a sum of about £120 was collected by Jones's friends after his death as a contribution to the £460 needed to buy 'a dwelling house and garden with a large frontage to the river, extending to the outer moat and immediately adjoining the Castle garden'. The house stood near, or on the site of, the present Wyndham block (*i.e.* the building of 1934 containing the military gallery) facing the nearby millstream. As it was stipulated by the subscribers to the Jones fund that some record of the gift be placed on the premises, it was decided to obtain a sarsen stone from Staple Fitzpaine to the

12.5: Jones's memorial plaque outside the Museum of Somerset. (AC)

south of Taunton.

Sarsen stones are blocks of silicified sandstone, probably of Tertiary age, of which many examples can be seen on this part of the Blackdown Hills.[190] The 5 feet high boulder was erected in the moat of Taunton Castle by the south west tower but in the refurbishment of the museum in 2010 and 2011 it was moved to a position adjacent to the main entrance. A plaque placed on the boulder bears the following inscription:

> This boulder From Staple Fitz-paine Records That a munificent Donation In aid of the purchase of The Castle grounds of the Somerset Archaeological and Natural History Society Was made by the friends of William Arthur Jones M.A. for 20 years one of its honorary secretaries as a Memorial of their respect for his talents and Esteem for his virtues.
> Ob. 23 Ap 1873 aet 54

12.6: A sarsen stone at Staple Fitzpaine. (AC)

Chapter 13
Postcript

WHEN WILLIAM ARTHUR JONES DIED IN APRIL 1873 he was survived by six of his eight children. His will appointed William Blake and the Revd John Robberds as his executors and his estate was valued at 'no more than £5000'. Household goods and furniture, plate, books, pictures, prints, philosophical (*i.e.* scientific) instruments and apparatus were to be held by trustees on behalf of the children for their use, and ultimately divided among them 'but at such period in such proportions and in such manner as such Trustees or Trustee at their or his discretion may consider most desirable'. Real estate and financial assets were to be handled at the discretion of the trustees. However, the main part of the will sets out the arrangements for the heraldic shields or coats of arms and coat of armour that he had been bequeathed by Edward Jarman of Brenley in Kent, William Blake's brother-in-law. These found their way to the Blake home at South Petherton and the shields are still in the family's possession.

The Jones children are listed in Appendix 2. Of those who survived their father the futures of four are of particular note. Margaret moved to Pau where she continued her father's interest in geology and, as we have seen, sent geological specimens to William Blake. She died there unmarried in 1880 aged 32. George Farewell wrote his father's original entry in the *Dictionary of National Biography* (revised by T.M. Mayberry for the *Oxford DNB*). He died after a short illness on 22 February 1926 in Mitcham in Surrey, having been a partner in the solicitors Soames, Edwards and Jones of the Strand, London. The Farewell Jones family lived in Cedar House in Mitcham for forty years and he was of sufficient importance in the town to have a street, Farewell Place, named after him. The youngest son, John Edward, became a civil engineer and, after working in India., retired to East Devon. More importantly for this story he wrote a long memoire in which many details of his father's life are given, albeit that his memory was occasionally faulty. Ellen, the youngest daughter, married her cousin William Farewell, son of William and Fanny Blake. Their grandson, W. Seymour Blake of South Petherton (born in 1919), made available much of the information on which this book is based.

When the Somerset Archaeological and Natural History Society celebrated its 50th anniversary in 1899 much was made of those who had contributed to its growth and increased status since its foundation in 1849.[191] However, in the report of the Society's *Proceedings* there is no specific reference to the very significant part played by Arthur Jones, despite the comment on his death that he had been 'one of the most valuable officers that this Society ever had'. Why this should be so is not obvious, but perhaps it was because he was not part of the 'establishment', being religously a Dissident and politically a Liberal. Later anniversaries also failed to mention him and his monument in the moat at Taunton Castle remained almost inaccessible and largely ignored for almost 140 years. The same might be said of Jones's contribution to the civic life of the town. There is a framed photographic portrait of him in the chapel in Mary Street but other than that he has been forgotten, even by local historians. A contemporary of Jones was Edward Jeboult, another key figure in Taunton's life whom he must have met, but a study published in 1983 of Taunton as it was in Jeboult's time makes no reference to the dissident Welshman among other significant local personalities of the time, despite his major contribution to the life of the town.[192]

Undoubtedly, William Arthur Jones was a major contributor to the development of the Somerset Archaeological and Natural History Society in its early days and a significant feature in Taunton's civic life from 1852 to 1873. As a geologist he could not be considered in the same league as, for example, Charles Moore, but his strength was a wide-ranging in natural history, history and archaeology which helped the Society to maintain its breadth of appeal. He deserves greater recognition both in the Society and in his adopted home town of Taunton. One hundred and sixty years after his death it is obviously difficult to say precisely how one would have reacted to him on a personal level. He was a good family man, appreciated as a minister by his various congregations and approachable, with a modicum of humour. However one senses that overall he might have been rather intense and perhaps not happy with idle chatter, but nevertheless probably good company.

Bibliography

A selection of the numerous publications used in the research for this book.

Carmarthen/Bridgend

Jones, E. Pan (1909): *Presbyterian College, Carmarthen – notable students 1796-1899.* (English title)

Jones, Gareth Elwyn (1994): *Modern Wales – A Concise History* (2nd ed.).

Morris, M.G. (ed.) (1998): *Romilly's Visits to Wales.*

Williams, H (1977): *Stage Coaches in Wales.*

Northampton

Ruston, Alan (1990): 'Unitarianism in Northampton – Rev. John Horsey to Sir Philip Manfield' in *Trans. Unitarian Historical Society*, vol. 19 no. 4 pp.238-251.

Glasgow

Boughey, Joseph (1994): *Hadfield's British Canals* (8th ed.).

Freeman, Michael and Aldercroft, Derek (1985): *The Atlas of British Railway History.*

Holt, Geoffrey O. (1986): *A Regional History of the Railways of Great Britain - Volume 10: The North West* (2nd ed.).

Martin, Don (1985): *The Forth and Clyde Canal- a Kirkintilloch View* (Auld Kirk Museum Publications No. 3 - Strathkelvin District Libraries & Museums).

Somerset.

Bush R. (1983); *Jeboult's Taunton.*

Bush R. (1994): *Somerset –A Complete Guide.*

Copp C.J.T., Taylor M.A., Thackray J.C. (1997): 'Charles Moore (1814-1881), Somerset Geologist' in *PSANHS* vol. 140 pp.1-36.

Friends of Banwell Caves Heritage Group (2004): *An outline history of Banwell Caves.*

Lawson-Clarke, Peter (1998): *The Blakes of South Petherton Through Six Generations.*

Mayberry, T. (1998): *The Vale of Taunton Deane.*

Murcheson (ed.) (1886): *Palaeontological Memoirs and Notes of the late Hugh Falconer AM, MD.*

Prudden (2001): *Geology and landscape of Taunton Deane.*

Runciman, Steven (1960): *The White Rajahs – a History of Sarawak from 1841 to 1946.*

South Petherton Local History Group (2000): *South Petherton in the Twentieth Century – a Village Album.*

Victoria County History of Somerset, Vol 4.

Webster C. and Mayberry T. (eds) (2007): *The Archaeology of Somerset.*

The Pyrenees

Baedecker (1914): *Southern France* (6th ed).

Bailey, Rosemary (2003): *The Man who married a Mountain.*

Belloc, H. (1909): *The Pyrenees.*

Bibliotheque Municipale de Pau (1995): *Les Anglais écrivent les Pyrénées (1739-1909)/Pyrenees as seen by British people (1739-1909).*

Dubin, Marc (1998): *The Pyrenees – the Rough Guide.*

Duloum, Joseph (1970?): *Les Anglais dans les Pyrénées et les Debuts du Tourisme Pyrénéen (1739-1896).*

Lefevre, Georges-Williams (1843): *The life of a travelling Physician from his first introduction to practice; including 20 years wanderings through the greater part of Europe* (in 3 volumes).

Martins, Charles, and Collomb, Edouard (1868): *Essai sur l'ancien glacier de la vallée d'Argelès.*

Mayoux, Philippe (2004): 'La Reforme en Bigorre, les Protestants de Bagnères' in *Bulletin de la Société Ramond,* 2004, pp21-70.

Mullen, Richard and Munson, James (2009): *'The Smell of the Continent' – the British Discover Europe.*

Le Memorial des Pyrénées (newspaper).

Mengelle, Agnes (2002*): Argelès-Gazost et ses environs.*

Musée Jeanne d'Albret, Orthez (2013: *Catalogue de l'exposition 'Pyrénéistes protestant au XIXe siècle'.*

Nicol, Antonin (1987): *Gavarnie.*

Pauli, Lori (2000): 'Lux Fecit: Farnham Maxwell Lyte, photographer' in *National Gallery of Canada Review,* Vol 1, 200.

Penck, Le Dr Albrecht (1883): *La periode glaciaire dans les Pyrénées* (Extrait des Miteilangen des Vereins fur Erdkunde zu Leipzig, traduit de l'Allemand par L. Braemer, Professeur a l'Ecole de Medecine de Toulouse).

Robb, Graham (2007): *The Discovery of France.*

Saint-Lebe, Nanou (2002): *Les femmes a la decouverte des Pyrénées.*

Saule-Sorbe, Helene (2004): 'Les Pyrénées Photographiées de Farnham Maxwell Lyte' in *Bulletin de Société Ramond,* 2004, pp.103-129.

Société d'Etudes des Sept Vallées Lavedan: *Bulletin.*

Société Ramond: *Bulletin* (various). (www.ramond-societe.com/les_bulletins.htm)

Taylor, Alexander (1842): *Climates for invalides: or, a comparative enquiry as to the preventative and curative influences of the climate of Pau, and of Montpellier, Hyeres, Nice, Rome, Pisa, Florence, Naples, Biarritz, etc. on health and disease* (1866 edition).

Tucoo-Chala, Pierre (1999): *Pau Ville Anglaise.*

Unitarianism

Chryssides, George (1998): *The elements of Unitarianism.*

Raymond, Jean and Pickstone, John V. (1986): 'The natural sciences and the learning of the English Unitarians' in Smith, Barbara ed.: *Truth, Liberty, Religion: essays celebrating two hundred years of Manchester College,* pp.127-184.

History of geological science

Barber, Lynn (1980): *The Heyday of Natural History 1820-1870.*

Cadbury, Deborah (2000): *The Dinosaur Hunters.*

McGowan, Christopher (2001): *The Dragon Seekers.*

Oldroyd, David (1996): *Thinking about the Earth: a History of Ideas in Geology.*

Thomson, Keith (2005): *The Watch on the Heath: Science and Religion before Darwin.*

Appendix 1

Key dates in Arthur Jones's life

1 May 1818	Born at Carmarthen
1834-1838	Student at Carmarthen College
1838-1841	Student at Glasgow University
Summer 1839	Does nine weeks 'supply' at Crewkerne chapel
April 1841	Takes up first ministry at Unitarian chapel, Northampton
9 June 1842	Marries Mary Cuff at Crewkerne
26 October 1842	Mary dies
March-July 1843	Travels through northern Europe
1 January 1846	Marries Margaret Blake at Taunton
Michaelmas 1849	Takes up post at Christ Church chapel, Bridgwater
1849	Joins the Somerset Archaeological and Natural History Society
September 1852	Takes up post at Mary Street chapel, Taunton
13 September 1853	Appointed general secretary of SANHS Natural History Department
3 Feb 1858	Elected Fellow of Geological Society
16 Sep 1860	Margaret, his second wife, dies
9 October 1864	Eldest son (Downing Blake) dies
17 Oct 1866	Leaves Taunton with family for Pyrenees
February 1867	Resigns post at Mary Street Chapel
15 June 1868	Daughter Mary dies in Montpellier
July 1868	Returns with family to Taunton. Lives at 3 The Crescent
27 Oct 1869	Elected Fellow of Ethnological Society of London
Early 1870	Moves to Tauntfield, South Road, Taunton
23 April 1873	Dies at Tauntfield

Appendix 2

The children of Arthur and Margaret Jones

Name	Born	Died (at)	Marital status
Downing Blake	16.10.1846	09.10.1864 Taunton	Unmarried.
Margaret	13.7.1848	22.03.1880 Pau	Unmarried.
Sarah Elizabeth	16.12.1849	22.10.1884	m. 5.8.1876: John Collins, son of Revd W.J. Odgers. Issue 1 son
William Arthur	8.5.1851	12.05.1890	m. 9.4.1878; Elizabeth Lang, daughter of Thos. Thomas. Issue 2 sons. 2 daughters.
Mary	11.12.1852	15.06.1868 Montpellier	Unmarried
George Farewell	27.1.1855	22.02.1926 Mitcham	Mitcham, Surrey m. March 1882: Anna Louisa, daughter of Chris. Jas. Thomas. Issue 2 sons, 3 daughters.
John Edward	19.1.1857	02.11.1938 Exton East Devon	m.18.11.1895: Kath. Ellen, daughter of Jno Thos. Reece. Issue 1 son.
Ellen	29.9.1859	11.02.1890	m. 08.02.1882: William Farewell son of William Blake. Issue 2 sons, 1 daughter.

Appendix 3

**Papers given by W.A. Jones to the Somerset Archaeological and
Natural History Society**

Date	Reference in the SANHS Proceedings	Title
1853	IV ii 44-59	*On Langport, the Llongborth of Llywarch, Hen's Elegy.*
1854	V i 19	*Conversazione* held at the museum in Nov 1853 *On Zoophytes, living and fossil; illustrated with many specimens of Actiniae and other Zoophytes, which were kept living for some months; and likewise by fossil specimens of corals etc. in the Museum*
1854	V ii 73	On the application of philology to archaeology.
1855	VI i 6/7	WAJ 'read the following notice of remains of Ancient British Hut-circles on Croydon Hill'.
1855	VI i 19	*Conversazione* held in Dec. 1854 *On Cephalopodes, recent and fossil, illustrative of objects in the Society's Museum.*
1855	VI ii 138	*On the geological formations in the neighbourhood of Dunster.*
1857	VII i 20	WAJ presented a transcript he had made of a parchment document in the Archives of the Corporation of Bridgwater.
1857	VII i 22	*Conversazioni* 19.11.55 *On the Microscope with some of its uses and revelations.* 21.1.56 *On the application of the Microscope to the investigation of Natural History and Archaeology.* 10.11.56 *The French Metrical System, and on an ancient seal discovered at Bridgwater.* 8.12.56 *On the Geological Formations in the neighbourhood of Taunton.* 9.3.57 *On the Collection of Bones of the Elephant, Rhinoceros, Tiger etc. in the Museum, from the Caverns of the Mendip Hills.*
1857	VII ii 25-41	*The Mendip bone caverns.*
1857	VII ii 100-104	*An inventory of vestments etc. belonging to Saint Katherine's Ile, in the church of Bridgwater, together with the rents.*
1858	VIII	*Conversazioni* 30.11.57 *On the Geology and Antiquities of the Mendips.* 22.3.58 *On the Fossil Reptiles of Somerset.*
1859	IX 43	*Conversazione* 14.11.59 *On the Old Library in the Close at Wells.*
1859	IX ii 128	*On the reputed discovery of King Arthur's remains at Glastonbury.*
1861	X 32	*Conversazioni* 21.1.61

1861 cont		*Historical Pictures of Taunton and the Neighbourhood.* 18.3.61 *Historical Pictures of Taunton no.2.*
1863	XI 54	*Conversazioni* 8.12.62: *On Ancient News Letters.* 2.2.63 *Historical pictures of Taunton Deane.*
1864	XII	*Conversazioni* 9.1.64: *On some Ancient British Coins.* 6.3.64: *On Volcanoes and Rocks of Volcanic Origin in the Quantock Hills.*
1865	XIII 30	*An account of the Beard collection of Mendip cave bones, with a scheme for purchasing them.*
1866	XIII 68	*Conversazioni* 9.11.65: *On the Ancient Sea Beaches and Sandbanks in the Lowlands, between Bridgwater and Langport, and the Submerged Forest on the north coast of Somerset.* 8.2.66: *On Ancient Roman Sepulchral Inscriptions.*
1868	XV ii 21	*Extracts from a MS of the borough of Axbridge.*
1869	XV	*Conversazioni* 22.2.69: *Historical sketches of Taunton: on the Western Circuit and the Assize held at Taunton AD1597-1600.* 29.3.69: *On the Danes in Somersetshire.*
1870	XVI	*Conversazioni* 12.12.70 *On the Castle and Manor of Taunton Deane.* 6.2.71 *On the Manor of Taunton Deane: its Lords and Customs.*
1870	XVI ii 55	*On Lord Chief Justice Dyer.*
1872	XVIII ii 77	*On the customs of the Manor of Taunton Deane.*
	XVIII ii *ad fin.*	*The Somersetshire Glossary.*

Appendix 4

Items given by WA Jones to the Taunton Museum

Sources:
1.   Museum of Somerset 2013 (MS)
2.   *Proceedings* of the Somerset Archaeological and Natural History Society (PSANHS)

Natural Science items

Date	Description	Source where known	MS ref. ref	PSANHS ref	Notes
	Smooth rupturewort	Lizard, Cornwall	593/1.2		
	Iron ore	Wookey	M.2807		
	Smithsonite	Mendip	M.2365		
1857	Trilobite	Llandeilo, Wales	5404	7 p.27	
1857	Trilobite	Llandeilo	5405	7 p.27	
1857	Trilobite	Llandeilo	5406	7 p.27	
1854	FOSSIL coral		97	5 p.16	
1854	SHELL Sepia sp. and Loligo sp., mounted in spirit		100	5 p.16	
1854	WORM indet. Annelid, described as Sea Mouse, Aphrodite sp		101a	5 p.16	
1857?	SLAG, CHARCOAL Metal smelting refuse		11956	7 p.27	
1857	MINERAL Unidentified iron and lead mineral		11955 98	7 p.27 5 p.16	
1854	FOSSIL *Sertulariae* mounted in spirit				
1859	FOSSIL *Icthyosaurus* fragments		11866	9 p.45	
1861	STONE Series of rock specimens illustrating the igneous formations of the Quantocks		11757	8 pp.33-36	
	FOSSIL Unspecified Silurian fossils		11953		
	INSECT Convolvulus Hawk-Moth		1859 11838	9 p.45	

Archaeological and related items

Date	Description	Source where known	MS ref.	PSANHS ref.	Notes
	Unidentified *Sestertius*	Blackey Tor, Dartmoor	3757/1990		
	Constantine 1 coin	Blackey Tor, Dartmoor	3758/1990		
	Constantine 1 coin	Blackey Tor, Dartmoor	3758/1990		
	Antoninus Pius Sestertius	Charterhouse on Mendip	856.N.1		
	Unidentified jeton 130/1992/35	Taunton			
	French jeton	Holway	130/1992/37		
	Romano-British (RB) sherds	Bishops Hull	A.3015		
	Knife blade	Charterhouse on Mendip	A.234		
	RB mortarium sherds	Norton Fitzwarren.	A.450		West Somerset Railway finds
	RB greyware sherd	Norton Fitzwarren			West Somerset Rrailway finds
	RB sherds (98)	Norton Fitzwarren	A.453		West Somerset Railway finds
	RB Jar rim sherd	Bishops Hull	A.625		
	RB Jar rim sherd	Bishops Hull	A.626		
	RB greyware bead rim sherds (2)	Bishops Hull	A.627		
	RB pot base	Bishops Hull	A.628		
	RB rim sherd		A.630		
	RB sherd	Bishops Hull	A.631		
	Late Neolithic beaker from	Brendley, Kent	A.958		Transferred to Maidstone Museum in 1989
	Clay tobacco pipe bowl	Charterhouse on Mendip	9/1998		
	Cooking pot sherd	North St, Taunton?	A.3089		
	Bronze handle (part only),	Bishops Hull	12055		
1866	Oak milking stool (badly fire damaged)	St James's Street, Taunton	B.640	14 p.69	'Dug from an old filled up water course under old houses'
	Brass rubbing from time of Edward II	St.Just, Cornwall	11831		

Items not in the Museum of Somerset records

Date	Description	PSANHS ref.	Notes
1854	1. An ancient Teapot with the legend 'No cider tax, apples at liberty'. 2. A record of the strong feeling to the 'cider duty' which prevailed in Somersetshire. 3. A curious candlestick used in Wales. 4. A series of Zoophytes, recent and fossil. 5. A collection of beetles and insects, from the interior of Africa.	SANHS 5 p18	Items given to form temporary museum at 6th Annual Meeting at Taunton
1861	1. 'The Battle of Sedgemoor, Rehearst at White Hall, a farce'.	SANHS 9 p30	Exhibited at the local museum, Langport, during the 13th Annual Meeting

Appendix 5

Description of the Chalet Lassalle, Argeles-de-Bigorre
From 'Three months in a French country house' by Margaret Jones, 1867

<u>Sunday 16 June 1867</u>

Excitement makes us get up early and we go out and inspect our new domain. The house is just as you enter the village high up just over the high road. It consists of downstairs first a little picturesque porch which leads into a little hall where there is a cupbirrors and two pictures wrapt from head to foot in thick white muslin. So perhaps underneath there is no picture at all or else one too ugly to be looked at!

From the drawing room a door leads into a sitting room, very pretty, in winter used as a dining room. The dining room is on your left as you enter the hall. It is a very ugly room all hung round with nails and hooks, for in winter it is used as the kitchen and the great open fire place with its dogs etc look just like a kitchen.

Upstairs over dining room is Papa's bedroom; over the drawing room is Sarah's and mine, such a splendid room after our little cabins at Pau. We have four windows, two to the east and two to the west, a large fireplace to the south and a door ditto and one door to the north - plenty of air! Two large beds and nice comfortable chairs. How delightful to stay here three months! In our room too there is a large cupboard full of books belonging to Madame Lassalle and she says we may get out what we want.

Our south door opens into Mary's and Nellie's room. They have two windows, one east one west, and a door opening south onto a sort of bridge which leads into another room built over a store house and in which room Edith sleeps. It is a very pretty room with a balcony to the east and south. Under Edith at the side of the storehouse is a little tiny room where Madame Lassalle lives, only just room for her bed, a chair and table - poor old creature what does she live in such a little hole for?

The boys sleep in the tower. I quite envy them for how practical and romantic it would be to sleep in the tower occupied by our own Black Prince. There is a flight of steps up to the first story which is a very nice bedroom in which Arthur will sleep when William comes. There is no window in this room, only a door with glass at the top. From this room is a flight of stairs all up to the top and no doors, so all gentlemen or all ladies must sleep in the tower. On the second story there is a wash room with tubs etc and on the third story a splendid bedroom where William is to sleep. It has three windows opening on to little balconies, one to the east one south and one north. Above this on the fourth story is the little boys' bedroom with two beds in it. How delighted John and Farewell are with their tower bedroom!

On the fifth story there is a little room with a table chairs and cupboard full of books - what a splendid place for study - and out of this little room you walk out onto the roof from which there is a most splendid view of the mountains and in the distance the white snow capped ones - oh it is splendid! One might spend hours on the top of the tower. I wonder if the Black Prince often went up there to see the view! Our kitchen is to the left of the tower very inconvenient so far from the house and Marie does not like it at all.*

*Marie - the maid who had come from Pau with the Jones family.

Source: Blake Archive.

Appendix 6

From the Church of England *Book of Common Prayer* (1662)

The Apostles Creed

I believe in God the Father Almighty, Maker of heaven and earth;
And in Jesus Christ his only Son our Lord, Who was conceived by the Holy Ghost, Born of the Virgin Mary, Suffered under Pontius Pilate, Was crucified, dead and buried: He descended into hell; The third day he rose again from the dead; He ascended into heaven, And sitteth on the right hand of God the Father Almighty; From thence he shall come to judge the quick and the dead.
I believe in the Holy Ghost; The holy Catholick Church; The Communion of Saints; The Forgiveness of sins; The Resurrection of the body, And the life everlasting. Amen.

The Athanasian Creed

Whosoever will be saved: before all things it is necessary that he hold the Catholick Faith.
Which Faith except every one do keep whole and undefiled: without doubt he shall perish everlasting.
And the Catholick Faith is this: That we worship one God in Trinity, and Trinity in Unity.
Neither confounding the Persons: nor dividing the Substance.
For there is one Person of the Father another of the Son: and another of the Holy Ghost.
But the Godhead of the Father, of the Son, and of the Holy Ghost, is all one: the Glory equal, the Majesty co-eternal.
Such as the Father is, such is the Son: and such is the Holy Ghost.
The Father uncreate, the Son uncreate: and the Holy Ghost uncreate.
The Father incomprehensible, the Son incomprehensible: and the Holy Ghost incomprehensible.
The Father eternal, the Son eternal: and the Holy Ghost eternal.
And yet they are not three eternals: but one eternal.
As also there are not three incomprehensibles, nor three uncreated: but one uncreated, and one incomprehensible.
So likewise the Father is Almighty, the Son Almighty: and the Holy Ghost Almighty.
And yet they are not three Almighties: but one Almighty./
So the Father is God, the Son is God: and the Holy Ghost is God.
And yet they are not three Gods: but one God.
So likewise the Father is Lord, the Son Lord: and the Holy Ghost Lord.
And yet not three Lords: but one Lord.
For like as we are compelled by the Christian verity: to acknowledge every Person by himself to be God and Lord;
So we are forbidden by the Catholick Religion: to say there be three Gods, or three Lords.
The Father is made of none: neither created, nor begotten.
The Son is of the Father alone: not made, nor created, but begotten.
The Holy Ghost is of the Father and of the Son: neither made, nor created, nor begotten, but proceeding.
So there is one Father, not three Fathers; one Son, not three Sons: one Holy Ghost, not three Holy Ghosts.
And in this Trinity none is afore, or after other: none is greater, or less than another.
But the whole three Persons are co-eternal together: and co-equal.
So that in all things, as is aforesaid: the Unity in Trinity, and the Trinity in Unity is to be worshipped.
He therefore that will be saved: must thus think of the Trinity.
Furthermore it is necessary to everlasting life: that he also believe rightly the Incarnation of our Lord Jesus Christ.
For the right Faith is that we believe and confess: that our Lord Jesus Christ, the Son of God, is God and Man.

God, of the Substance of the Father, begotten before the worlds: and in Man, of the Substance of his Mother, born in the world.

Perfect God, and Perfect Man: of a reasonable soul and human flesh subsisting;

Equal to the Father, as touching his Godhead: and inferior to the Father, as touching his Manhood.

Who although he be God and Man: yet he is not two, but one Christ;

One, not by conversion of the Godhead into flesh: but by taking of the Manhood into God;

One altogether, not by confusion of Substance: but by unity of Person.

For as the reasonable soul and flesh is one man: so God and Man is one Christ.

Who suffered for our salvation: descended into hell, rose again the third day from the dead.

He ascended into heaven, he sitteth on the right hand of the Father, God Almighty: from whence he shall come to judge the quick and the dead.

At whose coming all men shall rise again with their bodies: and shall give account for their own works.

And they that have done good shall go into life everlasting: and they that have done evil into everlasting fire.

This is the Catholic Faith: which except a man believe faithfully, he cannot be saved.

References

BA   Blake Archives
BL   Bodleian Library – Phillips-Robinson papers
CRO   Carmarthenshire Record Office
NRO   Nothamptonshire Record Office
ODNB   *Oxford Dictionary of National Biography*
PSANHS   *Proceedings of the Somerset Archaeological and Natural History Society*
SCG   *Somerset County Gazette*
SHC   Archives held in the Somerset Heritage Centre
TC   *Taunton Courier*
WAJ   William Arthur Jones
WAS   William Ayshford Sanford
WB   William Blake

Where a document provides several references only the first is usually given. Author references (e.g. Bush (1983)) relate to the bibliography.

[1] Quoted in Musée Jeanne d'Albret (2013).

[2] *TC* 26.11.1873.

[3] The entry for Jones in the original *DNB* was written by his son G.F. Jones and was revised for the *ODNB* edition by T.W. Mayberry.

[4] SHC, DD/SF/7/6/138.

[5] SHC, DD/FJ 15. The SHC contains two diaries written by Jones: 'Diary of the Fourth Session' whilst at Carmarthen College (SHC, DD/FJ 15) and a Glasgow diary (SHC, DD/FJ 16).

[6] N. Gibbard 'Heol Awst Congregational Church, 1703-1837' in *Carmarthenshire Antiquary* (2006), 5-15.

[7] Jones E.P. (1909), pp.54-5.

[8] CRO, CNC/42/58 Heol Awst chapel baptism register, 1792-1837.

[9] CRO, CNC/42/58 Heol Awst chapel baptism register, 1792-1837.

[10] Information from Bridgend Record Office, 2006.

[11] N. Gibbard 'Heol Awst Congregational Church, 1703-1837' in *Carmarthenshire Antiquary* (2006), 5-15.

[12] Inf. Dr William's Trust (www.dwlib.co.uk), 2009.

[13] SHC, DD/FJ 32. 'A Memoire' by Jones's youngest son John, *c*.1898. This appears to be a typed transcript in which occasional errors occur, particularly in relation to personal names in the Pyrenees.

[14] 'Eps.' – Epodes, a form of classical poetry.

[15] *PSANHS* 7, i, p.22.

[16] 'Cl. Fell' – class fellows; 'Organic remains' – fossils.

[17] See Yates's entry in the *ODNB*.

[18] National Library of Wales, E8/3/3/2.

[19] Probably *The Wisdom of God Manifested in the Works of the Creation* by John Ray (1627-1705), first published in London in 1691.

[20] BA, BFA BR 30 Margaret Blake to WB, 11.6.1844.

[21] 'Ap Morgan' of London, *Bridgend Sixty Years Ago* (*c*.1890). These are recollections of Bridgend in the 1830s, in contributions to the *Bridgend and Neath Chronicle* between February and April 1890. Ap Morgan was the author's pseudonym.

[22] BA, AFJ 1 P 'Descriptive Essay April 13, 1839'.

[23] Jones's route can be followed on O.S. Landranger Map Sheet 170 – Vale of Glamorgan West.

[24] BA, AFJ 1 M, John Jones to WAJ, 6.4.1838.

[25] Morris (1998), p.71.

[26] Williams (1977), pp.105-108. Williams' book includes graphic accounts of the difficulties of travel by stage coach at this time.

[27] BA, AFJ 1 Q, Samuel Cotton (Dr William's Trust) to WAJ, 24.10.1838.

[28] B. Richards, *Register of Swansea shipping* (www.swanseamariners.og.uk/shipsregister.php).

[29] Morris (1998), p.52.

[30] BA, AFJ 1 M, WAJ to John Jones, 15.1.1840.

[31] Swift boats were introduced on the canal in the early 1800s. The design of their hulls allowed them to travel at 10 mph rather than the usual 4 mph and gave a smoother ride. They were well-equipped to travel overnight and had sleeping accommodation: see Boughey (1994).

[32] Jones's route can be followed on O.S. Landranger Map Sheet 57 – Stirling and the Trossachs.

[33] The Antonine Wall from the Clyde to the Forth was built in A.D. 140 as a line of defence to the north of Hadrian's Wall. A turf wall on a stone base, it was abandoned twenty years later.

[34] See Walter Scott's poem, *The Lady of the Lake* published in 1810.

[35] From James Hogg, *Malise's Journey to the Trossacks*, quoted in E.A. Bohls and I. Duncan (eds), *Travel Writing 1700-1850, an Anthology* (2005), pp.177-180.

[36] SHC, D/Ncrew/4/3/2 Crewkerne Chapel

accounts.

[37] Lawson-Clarke (1998), p.34.

[38] BA, 19 d 1, WAJ to WB, 15.10.1839.

[39] *PSANHS* 47, i, p.239.

[40] BA, BFA BR1 30, Margaret Blake to WB, 11.11.1836.

[41] *PSANHS* 37, ii, p.60.

[42] BA, unnumbered, letter Mary Anning to WB, 17.3.1841.

[43] BA, WB's geology notebook, undated.

[44] R.J. Jones, *The Unitarian Students at the Presbyterian College, Carmarthen, 1796-1901* (1901).

[45] BA, BFA 19d 3, WAJ to WB, 13.4.1841.

[46] NRO, W.W. Laws, Map of Northampton, 1843.

[47] John Knox, the great Scottish protestant preacher (*c.*1514-72). Jones's reference to Knox is puzzling. The Glasgow University Archivist has commented on the diary entry as follows: 'It is most likely that William Arthur Jones is referring to the cap placed on graduates' heads at graduation by the Principal to award their degree. Perhaps he refers to John Knox as historically the graduation oath referred to the Church of Scotland. I have been unable to find any reference to the cap in our records during the 1840s, and I have also checked R.T. Hutcheson's book *Notes on academic dress in the University of Glasgow*, and again have not found any reference to the graduation cap for this period'.

[48] Ruston (1990), p.243.

[49] Both George and Anne Baker have entries in the *ODNB*.

[50] BL, c489/76, George Baker to Thomas Philips, 6.8.1845.

[51] BA, BFA 19d 2, WAJ to WB, 15.11.1839.

[52] BA, BFA 19d 3. Searches have failed to provide a definition for 'cowperite', but it is probably after the poet and hymn writer William Cowper (1731-1800), and in particular a reference to his poem 'Epitaph on a Hare', written in March 1873; presumably Jones was in sympathy with the sentiments expressed in the poem.

[53] BA, BFA BR1 30, WAJ to WB, 13.4.1841 Margaret Blake to WB, 1.9.1841.

[54] *Pers.comm.* Dr L. Sutcliffe, 1.5.2007.

[55] BA, BFA 19d 4, WAJ to the Blake family, 27.10.1842.

[56] BA, BFA 19d 5, WAJ to the Blake family, 27.1.1843.

[57] BA, BFA 19d 7, WAJ to WB, 20.7.1843.

[58] A photocopy of the passport is in SHC, DD/FJ 17; the whereabouts of the original is not known.

[59] BA, BFA 19d 7, WAJ to WB, 20.7.1843.

[60] Two of the places visited by Jones are now in the Czech Republic with different spelling: Teplitz is now Teplice and Tetschen has become Decin.

[61] See Sadler's entry in the *ODNB*.

[62] BA, AFJ 1 QBA, James Yates to WAJ, 4.8.1843.

[63] BA, AFJ 1 Q, copy of the chapel resolution,
.

[64] BA, AFJ 1 Q, WAJ to Revd J. Murch, 5.1.1845.

[65] BA, BFA 19d 3, WAJ to WB, 13.4.1841.

[66] BA, AFJ 1 Q, WAJ to Revd J. Murch, 5.1.1845.

[67] SHC, DD/FJ 17, Trustees of Northampton Chapel to WAJ, 27.6.1849.

[68] SHC, DD/FJ 17. Arthur's mother was probably now living with his brother John in Bridgend and was therefore easier to visit from Bridgwater than from Northampton.

[69] Census of Population, 1851.

[70] *Bridgwater Times* 17.2.1850; *PSANHS* 1, i, pp.127-139.

[71] Mayberry (1998), p.85.

[72] SHC, D/N/tau.mst/4/2/5, Mary Street Chapel committee minutes, 1843-1873.

[73] *Bradshaw's Railway Guide, 1863*.

[74] Unpublished paper by M. Siraut given to a SANHS meeting, 21.9.2013.

[75] *PSANHS* 1, p.2.

[76] *PSANHS* 5, i, p.8.

[77] *PSANHS* 7, i, p.22.

[78] *PSANHS* 7, i, p.22 also in SHC, DD/FJ 22.

[79] As in the case of W.A. Sanford's paper 'On Glaciers', given to a *conversazione* on 14.11.1859 and printed in the *TC* on 16.11.1859.

[80] *SCG* 17.9.1853.

[81] Bush (1994), p.129.

[82] *SCG* 21.11.1859.

[83] *SCG* 9.12.1854.

[84] *SCG* 5.12.1857.

[85] BL, c544 ff127-8, WAJ to Thomas Philips, 5.1.1857.

[86] W.A. Sanford, *Pleistocene mammalia of Somerset: illustrations of catalogue of bones in the Museum of the Archaeological and Natural History Society, Vol. 1, Felis* (1868).

[87] *PSANHS* 13, pp.119-245.

[88] Information from the Natural History Museum, 25 October 2007.

[89] 'Necrology of Brigham' in the *Collections of the Old Colony Historical Society*, Vol. 4 (Taunton, Massachusetts, 1889), pp.103-105.

[90] BA, BRI 51 H, Revd C. Brigham to WAJ, 12.7.1853.

[91] BA, BRI 51 H, Revd C. Brigham to WAJ, 12.7.1853..

[92] *PSANHS* 3, ii, pp.130-1.

[93] *PSANHS* 10, p.23; see also R.A. Croft (ed.), *Roman Mosaics in Somerset* (2009), p.25.

[94] SHC, DD/DN/651/56 WAJ to F.H. Dickinson, October 1861. A redrawing of the mosaic appears in Stephen R. Cosh and David S. Neal, *The Roman mosaics of Britain, vol. 2, South-West Britain* (2005), pp.282-287.

[95] See also Prudden (2001), p.71.

[96] SHC, SF 7/6/150, WAJ to WAS, 21.5.1860.

[97] *SCG* 23.11.1861. See also Somerset Historic Environment Record ref. 43398.

[98] *PSANHS* 11, p.33; see also *PSANHS* 133, p.57.

[99] D. Bromwich, 'Some visitors to Banwell Bone Cave' in *PSANHS* 154, pp.1-10.

[100] *PSANHS* 7, ii, pp.25-41.

[101] SHC, D/P/ban/23/25, Account of William Beard, Warden of Banwell Bone Caves, 1824-1865.

[102] SHC, DD/SAS c.1193/54.

[103] BA, AFJ 1 M, C. Brooke to WAJ, 8.7.1871.

[104] *PSANHS* 9, ii, p.151.

[105] Murcheson (1886), p.453.

[106] SHC, DD/SF 7/6/274, WAJ to WAS, 4.11.1865.

[107] BA, BFA 19d 11, WAJ to the congregation of Mary Street Chapel, 2.10.1866.

[108] BA, BFA 19d 11, WAJ to WB, 4.10.1866.

[109] SHC, DD/FJ 32, 'Memoire' by John Jones, 1896.

[111] Quoted in *Le Voyage en France Vol.1* (1995), pp.819-820.

[112] Quoted in Nicol (1987), p.64.

[113] The British interest in the Pyrenees is examined in detail in Duloum (*c*.1970) and Tucoo-Chala (1999); see also Mullen and Munson (2009) for a wider study of British tourists in nineteenth century Europe.

[114] Dubin (1998), p.336. This is a very crude figure as the proportion of foreigners increased considerably in the winter months, but it is clear that at least until the Franco-Prussian War (1871) the British (or English: the terms are often confused) formed the largest proportion of foreign visitors (Tucoo-Chala (1999), p.82).

[115] Quoted in a French translation Tucoo-Chala (1999), p.31; English original provided by the Royal Society of Medicine, London.

[116] Taylor (1842).

[117] Tucoo-Chala (1999), pp.5-6.

[118] Today, courtesy of Eurostar and the French TGV, one can leave London after breakfast and be in Pau in time for dinner, having had time for a good lunch in Paris *en route*. Alternatively, Pau is now directly connected by air to London (Stansted) Airport, which is having an effect on the numbers of British people visiting and buying property in the area.

[119] SHC, DD/SF 7/6/56, Herries Farquhar to WAJ, 15.8.1843. Herries Farquhar sent Jones whilst at at Bagneres-de-Bigorre £100 on behalf of his father.

[120] J. Miller, *Fertile fortune: the story of Tyntesfield* (2003), p.26.

[121] SHC, DD/FJ 19, Freeman to WAJ, 8.9.1867.

[122] *Baedecker's South of France* 6th ed. (1914), pp.141-144.

[123] *PSANHS* 7, i, p.22, reported in *SCG* 29.3.1856. See also 'Necrologie' of Lyte in the *Bulletin de la Societe Ramond*, pp.104-12 and in Saule-Sorbe (2004).

[124] *SCG* 27.1.1862.

[125] SHC, DD/SF 7/6/138, WAJ to WAS, 1.4.1867.

[126] BA, AFJ 1 M, Margaret Jones 'Three months in a French country house', unpublished (1867).

[127] SHC, DD/SF 7/6/138. Jones was not the only person to feel this way. The Englishman Charles Packe expressed similar views in a letter to his son (Duloum *c*.1970, p.485).

[128] SHC, DD/SF 7/6/138.

[129] BA, BRI 2 J: letters from Edith Blake to her mother, 1867.

[130] Lawson-Clarke (1998), p.70.

[131] SHC, DD/SF 7/6/138, WAJ to WAS, 1.7.1867.

[132] SHC, DD/FJ 22, Notebook of WAJ's visits to Burgos and Narbonne etc.

[133] G.E. Street, *Some Account of Gothic Architecture in Spain* (London, 1869), pp.2-3. The prime purpose of Street's travels in Spain was to visit and record in detail the major monuments of the country's Gothic architecture. However, the account of his visit to Burgos is full of fascinating reflections on the landscape, transport, food and culture of the area.

[134] Duloum (*c*.1970), p.293.

[135] Ecole des Hautes Etudes en Science Sociales, Paris.

[136] SHC, DD/SAS c.1193/61, WAJ to Badcock, 10.8.1867.

[137] SHC, DD/SF 7/6/138, WAJ to WAS, 1.4.1867.

[138] SHC, DD/SAS c. 1193/61, 10.8.1867.

[139] Achille Fould (1800-67) was born in Paris. He became Deputy for the Hautes-Pyrénées Département in 1842. In the Second Empire he was four times minister of finance. Outside politics he was a member of the Academy of

Fine Arts.

[140] 'M. Lyte' – Farnham Maxwell Lyte; 'M. Frossard' – Emilien Frossard.

[141] 'M. Packe' – Charles Packe.

[142] From the Journal of André Gide (1912), quoted in Bertrand Gibert, '*Protestantisme et Pyrénéisme*' in *Pyrénées Magazine* no. 147 (Mai/Juin 2013), p.68.

[143] Martins and Collomb (1868); SANHS Library, LP3 21.

[144] Louis Agassiz, *Etudes sur les Glaciers* (1840).

[145] SHC, DD/SF 7/6/138, WAJ to WAS, 1.7.1867.

[146] SHC, DD/SF 7/6/138, WAJ to WAS, 14.2.1868.

[147] SHC, DD/SF 7/6/138, WAJ to WAS, 14.2.1868.

[148] SHC, DD/SF 7/6/138, WAJ to WAS, 14.2.1868.

[149] Robb (2007).

[150] BA, BRI 3 C, WAJ's account book, 1866-1868.

[151] SHC, DD/FJ 32, John Jones 'Memoire', 1896.

[152] Lawson-Clarke (1998), p.21.

[153] SHC, DD/FJ 32, John Jones 'Memoire', 1896.

[154] SHC, DD/SF 7/6/138, WAJ to WAS, *c*.1869.

[155] SHC, DD/SF 7/6/138, WAJ to WAS, 1.7.1867. The Revd Frederick Brown of Clifton and W.F. Elliot of Taunton were both district / local secretaries of SANHS.

[156] SHC, DD/SF 7/6/138, WAJ to WAS, 15.6.1869.

[157] SHC, DD/SF 7/6/138, Hunt to WAS (?), 29.6.1869.

[158] BA, BFA 19d 17, WAS to WB, 6.4.1869.

[159] *PSANHS* 17, p.73.

[160] *PSANHS* 18, i, p.3.

[161] Bush (1983), p.73.

[162] *TC* 26.11.1873.

[163] *PSANHS* 4, ii, pp.44-49.

[164] *SCG* 8.8.1857.

[165] SHC, DD/FJ 18, correspondence between WAJ and the Charity Commision, 1855-1858.

[166] *SCG* 25.11.1855.

[167] *SCG* 26.4.1873.

[168] SHC, DD/SAS c.1193/61, WAJ to Badcock, 10.8.1867.

[169] See *SCG* 21.12.1872 for a full account of Jones's speech to the meeting.

[170] *SCG* 30.11.1857.

[171] *SCG* 5.12.1857.

[172] *PSANHS* VI, ii, p.138.

[173] *SCG* leading article 26.4.1873.

[174] *The Inquirer* 3.5.1873; *SCG* 3.5.1873.

[175] *SCG* 26.4.1873.

[176] SHC, DD/SAS c.1193/61, WAJ to WAS, 1.9.1867.

[177] SHC, DD/SF 7/6/138, WAJ to WAS, 31.12.1872.

[178] SHC, DD/FJ 24, letters from Margaret Jones (daughter of WAJ) to WB, Jan-Apr 1873.

[179] *TC* 30.4.1873.

[180] *SCG* 3.5.1873.

[181] *The Inquirer* 3.5.1873.

[182] *TC* 30.4.1873.

[183] *SCG* 13.12.1873.

[184] *SCG* 20.12.1873.

[185] *SCG* 20.12.1873.

[186] *PSANHS* 19, i, pp.2, 4.

[187] BA, unnumbered, King to WB, 11.9.1873.

[188] *PSANHS* 19, p.3.

[189] *PSANHS* 22, i, pp.3-4.

[190] Prudden (2001), p.90.

[191] *PSANHS* 54.i.12-13.

[192] Bush (1983).

Subscribers

The following people supported the publication of this volume by subscribing to the pre-publication offer:

Stephen Higgs, Churchinford

M.B. McDermott, Taunton

Dr A.J. Webb, Taunton

Mr Tim & Mrs Carole Lomas

Mrs Rosemary Chorley

Mr P. Ketley

Mr David Sutcliffe

Don Church, Ash Priors

Dr Michael G. Davies

Peter & Chris Jessop, Curry Rivel

David Clitheroe, Yarcombe, Devon

Dr Michael A. Taylor

John Clotworthy, Crewkerne

Revd W. John Young

Christopher Holme, Bristol